Co-Teaching in the
DIFFERENTIATED
CLASSROOM

Jossey-Bass Teacher

JB JOSSEY-BASS

Co-Teaching in the DIFFERENTIATED CLASSROOM

Successful Collaboration, Lesson Design, and Classroom Management

GRADES 5–12

Melinda L. Fattig and
Maureen Tormey Taylor

John Wiley & Sons, Inc.

Published by Jossey-Bass
A Wiley Imprint
989 Market Street, San Francisco, CA 94103–1741—www.josseybass.com

Readers should be aware that Internet Web sites offered as citations and/or sources for further information may have changed or disappeared between the time this was written and when it is read.

Limit of Liability/Disclaimer of Warranty: While the publisher and author have used their best efforts in preparing this book, they make no representations or warranties with respect to the accuracy or completeness of the contents of this book and specifically disclaim any implied warranties of merchantability or fitness for a particular purpose. No warranty may be created or extended by sales representatives or written sales materials. The advice and strategies contained herein may not be suitable for your situation. You should consult with a professional where appropriate. Neither the publisher nor author shall be liable for any loss of profit or any other commercial damages, including but not limited to special, incidental, consequential, or other damages.

Jossey-Bass books and products are available through most bookstores. To contact Jossey-Bass directly call our Customer Care Department within the U.S. at 800-956-7739, outside the U.S. at 317-572-3986, or fax 317-572-4002.

Jossey-Bass also publishes its books in a variety of electronic formats. Some content that appears in print may not be available in electronic books.

Library of Congress Cataloging-in-Publication Data

Fattig, Melinda L., 1972-
   Co-teaching in the differentiated classroom : successful collaboration,
   lesson design, and classroom management : grades 5–12 / Melinda L. Fattig and Maureen Tormey Taylor. — 1st ed.
       p.   cm.   —   (Jossey-Bass teacher)
   Includes bibliographical references and index.
   ISBN-13: 978-0-7879-8744-2 (alk. paper)
  1. Teaching teams.   2. Individualized instruction.   3. Lesson planning.   4. Classroom management.
5. Education, Secondary.   I. Taylor, Maureen Tormey, 1965- II. Title.
   LB1029.T4F38 2008
   373.11'48–dc22   2007031402

Printed in the United States of America
FIRST EDITION
PB Printing   10 9 8 7 6 5 4 3 2

Contents

To my incredibly supportive husband, Todd, and to my amazing children, Ashley and Trent. You are my daily inspiration. To my extended family for all the encouragement along the way. Finally, to former teachers Bonnie Gould and Jody Liss-Monteleone, who showed me the joys of teaching.

Melinda Fattig

To Bruce, for supporting me in pursuit of my dreams and for making me laugh along the way. To my parents, who always believe in me.

Maureen Tormey Taylor

Finally, we both dedicate this book to the students, families, and staff at McKinleyville Middle School, who unceasingly inspire and rejuvenate us.

Mindy and Mo

Preface

Historically, teaching has been an isolated profession: one teacher in one classroom with her students. A specialist pulled out the special education students for remedial lessons, and the gifted students were the responsibility of the general education teacher; or, if fortunate enough, the general educator might have consulted with a gifted education teacher.

At McKinleyville Middle School in northern California seven years ago, we decided that teaching and learning should not be business as usual. We were maintaining a system that was failing our children. General education teachers were trying their best, but not succeeding, to educate mixed ability levels in their classes. They lacked consistent support, using the only model they had ever known. After all, teaching has traditionally meant that the students' education was one teacher's responsibility and hers alone. We successfully changed that model.

Our Integrated Program

The change began by focusing on the special education students who were being taught in isolation, away from their peers. The dissatisfaction of a few teachers and the desire to do something about it led to development of a schoolwide, collaborative, co-teaching model (our Integrated Program), numerous presentations nationwide, and state and national recognition, all of which led ultimately to this book.

In 2004, we were selected by CalSTAT to be a Leadership School Site in the area of collaboration. Every year since, we have been selected as a Model Leadership Site in collaboration. In 2005, we were selected by the National Forum to Accelerate Middle-Grades Reform as one of four California schools that year to be a National School to Watch.

Students are no longer "Mrs. Taylor's" or "Mrs. Fattig's" but "ours." It is every teacher's responsibility to see that each child is receiving the best education he or she can, and we do that by collaborating, co-teaching, and differentiating lessons. In the wake of No Child Left Behind (NCLB) and high-stakes testing, teachers and administrators at McKinleyville Middle School, and at other schools across the nation, are making a difference. At P.S. 75

in New York City, for instance, the integration model and team teaching have proved to be extremely successful for both students and educators ("Learning-Disabled Students Blossom in Blended Classes," *New York Times*, Nov. 30, 2005).

We represent just a fraction of the teachers who choose this profession to make a difference in a child's life and inspire him, and we believe that all educators can and should use all of the available expert valuable resources—that is, one another—to make it happen for every student.

Purpose Of The Book

This book is written for teachers and administrators. It has two main purposes: to encourage and support educators who want to establish or improve a collaborative, co-teaching model serving students from special education to gifted; and to give educators tools and strategies for creating a differentiated classroom. We present practical tools and strategies for implementing a first-time co-teaching model. We also address the critical components of differentiated instruction and how to differentiate assignments on the basis of student needs. We include student profiles to illustrate the spectrum of learners, sample lessons, and templates that readers can either reproduce or adapt to meet their own needs and those of their students.

How This Book Is Organized

Co-Teaching in the Differentiated Classroom is organized into three parts. Readers can use individual sections or the book in its entirety. They can use it to improve their individual teaching practice or do so together with a community of educators.

Part One addresses collaboration in general and specifically prepares teachers to co-teach. In Chapter One, we share how our special education program evolved from an unsuccessful traditional one to a successful integrated program. Mindy Fattig shares her perspective as a special education teacher, and Maureen Taylor shares her perspective as a general education teacher. Chapter Two covers such partnership essentials as establishing common expectations, classroom management, flexibility, planning, and scheduling.

Part Two addresses the Differentiated Instruction model that we have successfully implemented, largely on the basis of our studies of Nancy Craig, Carol Ann Tomlinson, and Rick Wormeli. In Chapter Three, we cover the basics of differentiation, methods for getting to know the students, community building activities, and developing student profiles. In Chapter Four, we share planning strategies for designing differentiated lessons and questions and for achieving flexible grouping. Chapter Five introduces tiered assignments; shows how to adapt curriculum to meet student needs; and offers sample lessons, activities, and templates. Chapter Six offers a variety of sample student contracts and menus, and Chapter Seven discusses assessment as a grading tool.

Part Three introduces the essentials for implementing a schoolwide program. Chapter Eight emphasizes the need for administrative support and can be useful to teachers and administrators alike who are seeking to foster a more collaborative climate at their site or to meet the needs of all of their students within general education classes by implementing an integrated co-teaching model. Chapter Nine describes other key ingredients that can help promote a successful change effort.

Parts One and Two end with "exit cards," our effort to support you in reflecting on your own teaching and learning. They are versions of the student exit cards used in the classroom as an assessment tool (see the explanation of their use in Chapter Four).

Throughout the book, we have included testimonials from various teachers who differentiate instruction in a co-teaching classroom. We have included student anecdotes that we believe represent typical classroom scenarios educators must deal with daily, and we explain how we have handled such situations ourselves.

In the back of the book, we provide a glossary for quick reference to terms that we use regularly, as well as an annotated bibliography of the resources most influential on our thinking and on our applications.

It is our greatest hope that readers of this book will be encouraged to turn to their colleagues—the true experts in the field of education. We are our own greatest resource for creative and innovative approaches to meeting the needs of all students. It is our responsibility—and indeed a privilege—to experience and model for children the joys of teaching and learning together as a community.

Acknowledgments

Co-Teaching in the Differentiated Classroom, although written by just two authors, is truly the work of many. Christie Hakim and Julia Parmer, educational editors at Jossey-Bass, have been patient and giving by coaching us through production of our first book. We also thank copyeditor Thomas Finnegan for putting it all together so seamlessly, and Justin Frahm, our production editor, for his understanding and flexibility. Other educators and educational organizations have influenced us in many ways and have certainly brought us to this point:

The National Writing Project, and our local site the Redwood Writing Project, whose fundamental philosophy is "teachers teaching teachers"

Carol Ann Tomlinson, on differentiated instruction

Marilyn Friend, on collaboration

Jay McTighe and Grant Wiggins, on Universal Backwards Design (UBD)

Richard DuFour on collaboration and professional learning communities

Rick Wormeli, on the workings of a differentiated classroom

Nancy Craig, Gifted and Talented Education Coordinator of Sacramento City Schools, on differentiated curriculum design

California Services for Technical Assistance and Training (CalSTAT)

CalSTAT is a special project of the California Department of Education that helps schools and families educate children and young adults with special needs. In part they identify and award exemplary California schools and districts. The staff and students at McKinleyville Middle School are extremely thankful for all the support and resources that CalSTAT has provided in assisting us to become and remain a State Model Leadership site in the area of special education and general education collaboration.

In addition, trainings by Steve Zuieback on system change, Kevin Feldman in literacy, and Jeff Sprague in behavior have transformed our school and helped us achieve recognition as a National School-to-Watch Model Middle School.

We thank the McKinleyville Union School District for its ongoing support and encouragement every step of the way during our evolution. We are particularly thankful for the generosity, advice, and enthusiasm of our very own Gifted and Talented Education Coordinator Nancy Wheeler.

Finally, the staff at McKinleyville Middle School has inspired us every day. Through their continued commitment to impart not just a quality education but an *exceptional* one for all students, we were encouraged to write this book and hopefully inspire (and furnish tools and strategies for) educators across the nation.

The Authors

*M*elinda (Mindy) Fattig earned her B.A. in liberal studies at Humboldt State University (California) and her teaching credentials at California State University, Chico. She is currently working toward a master's in special education at Humboldt State. Mindy was awarded the Humboldt County Teacher of the Year in 2006.

Maureen Tormey Taylor earned her B.A. in history at the University of California, Berkeley, and a master's in education and teaching credentials at Stanford University. Maureen was honored as McKinleyville Union School District Teacher of the Year in 2002.

Together, they share twenty-five years of teaching experience. Mindy spends her spare time with her husband, Todd, and her two children, Ashley and Trent. Maureen spends her spare time with her husband, Bruce, and their dog, Maggie.

Part One

Collaboration and Co-Teaching

Chapter One

Why Collaborate?

Collaboration is no longer a choice; it is a necessity.
Working together. . . is essential in order to address
the increasingly diverse and sometimes daunting
needs of students. If we work together, both when it is
easy and when it is difficult, we can meet these needs.

Marilyn Friend, University of North Carolina

Collaboration involves planning, learning from one another, and taking small steps toward a more integrated co-teaching model. Collaboration can happen among a team of educators, an entire staff, or simply between two teachers. Regardless of how many are involved, our primary goal is always to increase and ensure student learning. In his book *On Common Ground: The Power of Professional Learning Communities,* Richard DuFour asserts that educators can help every student achieve high-level learning only if we work together collaboratively (DuFour, Eaker, and DuFour, 2005). In 2005, Valerie Chrisman investigated why only 83 of 430 identified low-performing schools in California (under No Child Left Behind) managed to sustain growth in test scores over two years. She discovered that one consistent factor contributing to success in those schools was the regular use of collaboration time that administrators gave to teachers (Chrisman, 2005).

We have found that any combination of teacher teams, whether of general educators, special educators, paraprofessionals, or a mixed pair, can plan and share expertise with great results. For example, as the special education teacher Mindy brings her special education expertise to the general education classroom. She knows what her students with learning disabilities need in terms of their learning goals, and the curriculum modifications that will help get them there. Maureen, as the general education teacher, is the curriculum expert who knows what standards all students must meet in her particular content area. She is familiar with what types of lessons have been successful in the past and which ones require modification. During every planning session, whether for one lesson or an entire unit, we learn from one another and continue to evolve as teachers. An unintentional but welcome outcome of this arrangement has been rejuvenation and truly joyful teaching.

"Collaborative conversations," writes DuFour (2005), "call on team members to make public what has traditionally been private—goals, strategies, materials, pacing, questions, concerns, and results. These discussions give every teacher someone to turn to and talk to, and they are explicitly structured to improve the classroom practice of teachers—individually and collectively."

What is Co-Teaching?

We define co-teaching as two credentialed teachers teaching together at the same time in the same classroom. Any pair or group of people can collaborate without co-teaching, but effective co-teaching cannot exist without collaboration.

In our case, one teacher is a special education (SE) teacher and the other a general education (GE) teacher. Co-teachers decide together what students should know, understand, and be able to do, and they plan lessons as partners. The advantages are clear:

- Downsizing an overcrowded classroom
- Managing behavior challenges
- Designing curriculum to meet a greater variety of student needs
- Sharing various classroom responsibilities, including grading, providing feedback to students, and communicating with families
- Modeling teamwork for students

Through trial-and-error, we have found what works best for our students and for us as teachers. Our instinctive evolution parallels the recommendations produced in research done by Marilyn Friend:

- Co-teaching a whole class lesson
- Each teacher working with a predetermined small group (variety of models used; see "grouping")
- Both teachers assisting students who need help during independent work time
- Both teachers holding individual conferences with students, such as during writing workshop

- Separating the class into two, each partner teaching a lesson (same or different) to one-half of the class

- One teaching a whole class lesson while the other performs a variety of duties, including but not limited to teaching one-on-one, assessing, grading, planning, and so on

The Benefits of Working Together

Anyone who has ever been part of a team knows that working together is vital to the success of all. Our experience with collaborating and co-teaching has further validated this philosophy.

We are middle school teachers in rural northern California who began collaborating in 2001 at the Redwood Writing Project Summer Institute. Mindy, a special education teacher, had spent the previous school year piloting an integrated core program at McKinleyville Middle School. Maureen had recently been informed that she would be the next GE core teacher to work with an SE teacher the following year. Our collaborative efforts began that summer at the Summer Institute and during an invaluable district-sponsored in-service on differentiation with Nancy Craig, whose job title is gifted and talented education (GATE) coordinator for the Sacramento City Schools. Over the ensuing years, a respectful partnership evolved, and we began to share our story and our strategies with other educators in Humboldt County. Following a presentation at the National Association of Supervision and Curriculum Development in New Orleans in the spring of 2003, we were struck by how many educators left wanting to know still more about our experiences. Half-joking, Mindy said, "We should write a book!" This is the product.

We do not claim that the information here is new. However, it offers a fresh perspective on best-practice teaching that benefits every member of a learning community—students; veteran, aspiring, and new teachers; paraprofessionals; and administrators. Some educators have pointed out that collaboration and co-teaching is too costly, too time-consuming, or simply not for them. But on a practical level, such collaboration and co-teaching naysayers cannot deny that engaged learners retain information, and it logically follows that they will perform better on assessments. At McKinleyville Middle School, for instance, our state scores have continuously increased since we started our collaboration model. In our opinion, the practice of teaching through collaboration and differentiation has even more valuable long-term benefits: bringing to students a curriculum that is accessible and challenging, and learning experiences that nurture a lifelong love for learning.

Developing differentiated units and lessons does require time and creative energy, which a single teacher may rarely possess in the current educational climate. It makes perfect sense, therefore, to team up and share with another. Furthermore, working together in differentiation of curriculum is more important now than ever:

○ High Objective Uniform State Standards for Educators (HOUSSE) require veteran teachers to demonstrate subject matter competence in alignment with No Child Left Behind legislation (NCLB Reauthorization, 2006).

○ Districts are mandated by NCLB to meet benchmark standards.

○ "The No Child Left Behind Act neither excludes nor includes gifted learners (National Association for Gifted Children, 2003), encouraging many states to compromise services for the gifted in order to focus on specific mandates addressed in the legislation" (*Roeper Review*, 2006). For the most part, servicing gifted needs is left to the discretion of the local education agency, which makes it all the more crucial that we as professionals take on the responsibility of servicing them.

○ In accordance with the Individuals with Disabilities Education Act (IDEA Reauthorization, 2004), educators are required to offer instruction for special education students in the "least restrictive environment," to the maximum extent that is appropriate.

○ According to the Five Core Propositions of the National Board (www.nbpts.org), "Teachers are members of learning communities," and "Accomplished teachers contribute to the effectiveness of the school by working collaboratively with other professionals on instructional policy, curriculum development, and staff development."

Mindy's Story: One Special Education Classroom

This is a story of one teacher's evolution—my evolution—over the past seven years. At one point in my career, I heard comments being made every day, sometimes aloud by students in my class but more frequently on the playground by their peers:

"This class sucks!"

"I don't care. I'm in the 'special' class."

"Hey, retard!"

It occurred to me by day three in my new position as a resource core teacher in a traditional pull-out program that this was a ridiculous idea: place all the identified learning-disabled students in grades six through eight in the same room and teach them.

"You're supposed to have those kids."

"You're the specialist."

"I don't know how to help them."

These comments were from my fellow teachers, who knew only that the SE teacher was supposed to teach a certain group of students. Apparently, in this system, educating these students was my responsibility and mine alone. I needed support, any support, but I feared that my experience and ability would come into question. It must be my fault, not the system's, that I hate this job, right?

Only fifteen or thirteen kids in one room at a time! Sounds great in theory. I mean, we even had a paraprofessional. But of the twenty-eight students I had, one was reading only a year below grade level and the rest were two to four years below in reading and writing. Two were labeled emotionally disturbed, and most of them had been in some facet of special education for at least two or three years. They had mastered the attitudes that the labels "stupid," "retarded," and "special" earned them. Top this off with the hormones and peer pressure of middle school, and our classroom was a minefield ready to explode every day. It took every ounce of my energy to maintain control of the students. Never mind that the seventh and eighth graders bragged endlessly that they had gotten the last teacher fired, and that my paraprofessionals kept quitting!

Worst of all was the realization that I was turning into the teacher that I swore I would never become. I hated myself for it. I had always wanted to be a teacher who reached the "hard to teach." I had always strived to be a teacher from whom kids would learn not only skills but also life lessons. I had always dreamed of inspiring them as my teachers always inspired me. Instead, I began to fill the detention room with "my" kids. I became a reactive teacher instead of a proactive one. This was not fun, it was not enjoyable, and I knew it was not beneficial for the students or me.

Colleagues and parents, however, gave glowing reviews of my job performance, since the "resource" students were not seen very much in the principal's office. But by my own internal standards of measuring my success and that of the students I taught, my performance was far from even satisfactory. I knew these kids needed to experience success. I knew that at their age they absolutely needed to be with their peers, the ones who have the greatest impact on adolescent choices. These students, restricted to a class in the "portables," deserved and needed to participate in all the exciting curriculum activities just as their peers did. I needed to find a way for them to feel good about themselves. I wanted them to want to go to school, stay in class, and succeed. Why would they need any less than what I wanted for myself? I realized that my next, real challenge would be to convince GE teachers of my beliefs even though they were so accustomed to having the students with learning disabilities somewhere else.

Though I feared he would think I was incompetent, I decided I had to share my frustrations with my principal, Dale McGrew. I took a deep breath and with poise walked into his office and said all in one rush, "These kids deserve better. These kids are not working up to their ability because the environment that we have created for them, in their mind, confirms that they are stupid. I am exhausted mentally and physically, and I am doing all I can to redirect behaviors. I know I am a good teacher and I know I can do a great job, but right now I hate the teacher I have become."

Amazingly, he asked, "What do you suggest?"

I was stunned. The words echoed in my mind. I had no clue, but I did know I was determined to give him the best answer I could. I had research to do.

Through an Internet search and good fortune, I came across California Services for Technical Assistance Training (CalSTAT). At their annual conference, I was introduced to schools that were already successfully collaborating. I now had real models we could aspire to emulate. With Dale's never-ending support and encouragement, I continued to research schools and to gather more detailed information.

The real turning point came at the California League of Middle Schools annual conference in San Francisco, which I attended with six other teachers from my school site. One night after the conferences, I was talking with Julie Giannini-Previde, an eighth grade GE teacher from my school. I explained my frustrations with our current special education program and how I was trying to develop a more effective program for the students with learning disabilities. I shared the research from CalSTAT on their collaboration models. Julie had taught in a similar program at her previous school and it was quite successful. Then she said something amazing, a comment that made all the difference and made our program what it is today: "I'd be willing to have the resource students in my class and team-teach." Half my battle was won. I had a general education teacher who wanted "my kids" and was willing to co-teach with me. My students and I would finally get out of the portables and join the rest of the school!

We developed and piloted the Integrated Resource Model for our school after planning through the remainder of that year, attending more conferences, and researching Paradise Unified and Elk Grove schools in California, all of which used a collaborative model for special education. Because the majority of the resource students were in eighth grade, we distributed my eighth grade core load between Julie's two core classes. All of the students were now "our" students. Right from the beginning, we made it clear that the students have two teachers, plain and simple. This is the model we use throughout the school today.

In the first year, the results—both academic and behavioral—were astonishing. Detentions were down 66 percent and suspensions reduced 50 percent for the same group of kids. Three-fourths of the learning-disabled students mastered their academic goals and objectives, compared to 45 percent the previous year. In a tribute to that success, the resource students were happy! I could see smiles on their faces as they played basketball with their peers. I could see them joking around in class and having fun, yet not being afraid or intimidated to ask a classmate for help on an assignment. I evolved from despising both the teacher I had become and the students I taught to wanting to do nothing other than work with these kids. I was excited to see the smiles on their faces as they realize again and again that they can do the work and that they are indeed capable in their own eyes. This is why I became a teacher. This is why I now love my job.

Maureen's Story: One General Education Classroom

By the end of the 2001 school year, after eight years of teaching middle school language arts and social studies, I realized that, although I was practicing all the techniques I had always believed constituted "good" teaching (including questioning through the various levels of Bloom's taxonomy and grouping heterogeneously as advocated by Howard Gardner), there were times when my students still failed. I spent endless hours creating "stimulating" and "fun" projects that were high-level and challenging. I gave specific directions for students to follow, clear expectations, and extensive written feedback on work they produced. I was (shamefully) considered a "great teacher" by parents, colleagues, and students because of the high standards I set. I did not want to blame "lazy" kids, "careless" parents, or previous teachers for not adequately preparing students. I wasn't satisfied with my teaching, nor with my students' learning—or apparent lack thereof. I have always believed that every student can, and more important wants to, learn. So why were they successful sometimes and unsuccessful at other times? I was determined to find some answers. I also needed to find answers because I was slated to participate in an integrated core program the following school year.

Most educators believe, and we all very likely embrace, the philosophy that every student can learn and ideally will be a lifelong learner. By the summer of 2001, however, I realized that unless we really know what works best for each of us as unique learners, simply knowing and practicing what the educational pundits expound, what the state expects, and what the school districts proclaim as their mission is not enough. What educators need to know is how

Tyson can learn, how Ashley can learn, and how Jake can learn. These three students and I shared a common seventh grade classroom. But one of them was reading at seventh grade level, another at second grade, and the third at post-high school level. I needed to make it my mission to more actively personalize my teaching and my students' learning.

Since 1998, I had been actively involved in our local National Writing Project site, the Redwood Writing Project. In 2001, the year in which my transformation began, I participated in the annual summer institute. As luck would have it, Mindy Fattig, my school's learning disabilities specialist, was also participating in the institute. I knew that she had just completed a year of piloting the Integrated Resource Program with great success, and I was anxious to prepare for my own upcoming experience in the fall. Together with another valued colleague, Ellen Krohn, we discussed our common frustrations and collaborated daily.

Throughout the summer institute, I borrowed and bought all the books and articles I could find about differentiation by Carol Ann Tomlinson and Diane Heacox, among others. I recognized that differentiation isn't anything new. It is simply a philosophy about effective teaching and learning. It involves many of the good teaching practices I had been applying up to this point. I realized that I simply needed to become more purposeful in their application. Differentiation and truly effective teaching involve recognizing that every student comes to us at a unique starting point. Indeed, even the Reading/Language Arts Framework for California Public Schools, adopted by the California State Board of Education and published by the California Department of Education in 1999, "assumes that all learners will work towards the same standards yet recognizes that not all learners will acquire skills and knowledge at the same rate." In addition, the framework "addresses the full range of learners in classrooms" and goes on to list the various types of learners educators know personally in their classrooms from day to day and year to year: "English learners, special education students, students with learning difficulties, and advanced learners." Until this time, I had too often assumed that all students would come to me prepared to be successful seventh grade students. I was now rethinking this assumption and embracing a more realistic philosophy about teaching and learning.

I was also inspired every day by collaborating with Ellen and Mindy, and I felt recharged for the new school year. By the end of the summer, Mindy, Ellen, and I had developed a differentiated reading program for a mixed-ability middle school classroom. Differentiation truly spoke to me as I recalled the reason I went into teaching in the first place: to make learning a joyful experience for children.

In the fall of 2001, I was no longer simply a GE teacher. I still taught seventh grade reading, language arts, and social studies in my core class, but that year I co-taught an integrated core class with special education teacher Holly Matthews. Her students with learning disabilities were fully mainstreamed into the general education program, and now these kids were part of our class. They were our kids.

The road to achieving what I would consider to be the ideal differentiated teaching and learning classroom is ever evolving. Yes, it is hard work and time consuming. But as an educator, I believe it is my responsibility to constantly question and challenge my methods if I am going to make learning meaningful for every child. It is crucial, and it is definitely doable if we reflect on and share our successes and failures with one another—and most important, if we collaborate. My first years of actively differentiating spelling, reading, and writing could not have been as successful as they were had it not been for my partnership with Holly, my collaboration with colleague Anne Hartline in our peer reading program, and my work with student teachers Cassandra Korp and Elizabeth Claasen. It is the inspiration from others, especially Mindy Fattig and Julie Giannini-Previde, the team that piloted our school's Integrated Resource Program, which has led me to this point in my teaching.

In the same way that we strive to give our students daily opportunities in the classroom that allow them to search, find, question, grapple, fail, and succeed in their learning, educators too must constantly look for and discover ways to improve teaching and learning.

Our Integrated Classroom

In the spring of 2002, we became a seventh grade integrated core team when Mindy's sixth grade learning-disabled students looped up a grade level with her. We agreed that co-teaching was one of the best things that had ever happened to us in our professional careers.

Despite Mindy's best efforts when she was alone in her traditional, isolated setting, she had felt frustrated by her students' lack of success: "These were good kids—I truly believed that. They deserved the best possible education and I did not know how to provide it. I had run out of 'expert' books and ideas. The ones acting out constantly overshadowed the ones who wanted to learn. The higher-skilled kids were bored, and the lower-skilled kids were frustrated because I was forced to teach to the bulk of the kids in the middle." Now, together, we determine what we want students to learn, how they will learn it, how we will know they have learned it, and what we do when they don't.

In our integrated classroom, not only is there often more than one adult in the room with some thirty students but there is a certain energy that was, until now, lacking. Together we are excited over new ideas. We are able to share frustrations together. We can solve problems together. We celebrate successes together. Enthusiasm infuses every planning session from the outset. To this day, it hasn't waned.

Chapter Two

Partnership Essentials

Even teachers reluctant to participate in a co-teaching partnership cannot deny the benefits of sharing expertise and lowering student-teacher ratios. No matter the feelings about sharing students and classroom space, teaching is about students and their learning. If nothing else, co-teachers hold in common the fundamental value of education. Begin by getting to know one another's personalities, sharing your goals, your teaching styles, and your preferences, as well as expectations on classroom behavior and student performance. Open and honest discussion about these fundamentals of daily classroom operation fosters a working relationship built on trust and understanding.

The night Mindy and Julie discovered their common interest in integrating SE students into the GE class, their relationship bloomed.

> We [Mindy and Julie] talked for hours that night, getting to know each other professionally and personally. Over the course of our conversation, I realized that Julie and I have similar personality traits that lent themselves to a natural match in starting this endeavor. We both are tremendously hard workers, willing to put in time and energy above and beyond the regular school day. We believe in consistency and high expectations, but we also agree that students and teachers must have mutual respect and trust. Most importantly, we truly believe that all students can succeed in a general education classroom.

Whether or not you are just beginning with collaboration or co-teaching, the advantages are apparent from the start. Throughout our own evolution and during countless workshops with educators throughout the nation, we have determined a number of requirements for both successful collaboration and implementation of a co-teaching program:

- Establishment of common expectations
- Shared responsibilities
- Flexibility
- Planning
- Coordinated scheduling
- Administrative support for teachers

Establishing Common Expectations

Just as Julie and Mindy did when they were first starting out, co-teachers must establish common expectations for professional conduct and student behavior and performance. For instance, before co-teaching, the primary goals of the special education (SE) teacher may be to support the general education (GE) teacher and ensure that her students with individual education plans (IEPs) are making progress. Once co-teaching has been implemented, both teachers want the same thing: to challenge and prepare all of their students to achieve maximum learning potential and ultimately grade-level standards. The GE teacher must provide the SE teacher with the information she needs to feel comfortable, for instance walking into the shared class in the middle of an ongoing lesson and modifying curriculum; taking over teaching a whole class lesson; or working with a small group for enrichment, preteaching, or reteaching. The SE teacher needs to feel comfortable walking into the integrated classroom and teaching in a variety of situations. Likewise, the GE teacher needs to feel comfortable sharing instructional responsibilities.

Through constant communication, the partners establish mutual trust. True partners recognize that if the other is unavailable to teach at a given time, it is for a good reason. For example, if Mindy has an IEP meeting, Maureen teaches, modifies, or works with small groups. If Maureen needs to meet with a student one-on-one to discuss behavior modification, Mindy teaches, modifies, or works with small groups. Co-teaching partners share virtually all the responsibility of running a classroom: planning lessons, assessing student progress, conferencing with students. Communication and flexibility make a team particularly successful.

Initially, because the GE teacher is the content area specialist, she may serve as the primary curriculum instructor. Meanwhile, the SE teachers' role may be that of support provider, specifically for those students with IEPs. Over time and depending on the teachers' level of comfort, those roles become less clearly delineated. In our situation, our ultimate goal was for teachers to play equal roles, serving all students regardless of achievement level, learning style, or IEP. Students in our classes recognize that they have two teachers. Period. There is no special ed or general ed teacher. Nor do they associate themselves with one category or the other. We believe this is one of the greatest outcomes of having implemented the integrated special education program.

As educators in our respective teaching specialties, we know what we need and what our students need. It is therefore our responsibility to share our strengths and weaknesses with all our partners. As we like to say, "Check your ego at the door!" Because our purpose as educators is to help and support children, it is our responsibility to seek out new knowledge from our partners, to see change as being positive for us and for our students.

Establishing expectations is a critical initial step when you begin working in any co-teaching situation. In more than one workshop, we have heard from teachers expressing frustration that the needs of their students are misunderstood, that their own needs as teachers are not respected, and that the partnership was a complete failure. It is therefore well worth your time to sit down with your partner from the get-go, whether you are strangers or best friends, and discuss your expectations for how the partnership will be successful for both of you and for your students.

It is easiest to begin with the basics: classroom management. Share your philosophies and expectations for student behavior and general procedures. How should students enter and exit the room? What will the allowable noise level be? May students go to the bathroom, sharpen pencils, and get water during class?

Scenario

Ten minutes before class ends and immediately after an assignment has been given, Dean asks Mrs. Williams if he can go to the bathroom. She knows that he often procrastinates and uses a trip to the bathroom (or the water fountain, or the pencil sharpener) to avoid doing his work. She therefore asks Dean, "Can you wait just ten more minutes?" He sighs, "Yeah," and returns to his desk. As she leans over to help another student, Dean approaches Mr. Hoffman and says, "I really need to go to the bathroom. . ." and he lets him go. Dean takes the last eight minutes of class walking extremely slowly to and from the restroom.

This situation, in which students "play" the two teachers, is one many of us have experienced. They will test you at first, but with common expectations in place students quickly realize that you and your partner are on the same page.

Establish expectations regarding curriculum next. Keeping in mind that our purpose as educators is to ensure maximum, high-quality learning for every student, it is critical that we understand our own weaknesses and limitations. Imagine being reassigned by your administrator to teach a new class. You have to brush up on the curriculum before you teach it for the first time. Along the same lines, you must be willing to prepare to take on a co-teacher's responsibilities. Mrs. Williams, the SE teacher, needs to brush up on her biology, and Mr. Hoffman, the GE teacher, has to learn how to modify curriculum to meet the IEP goals of individual students. They help each other be successful, just as they would help their students. Push yourself to learn the new subject matter, just as you would push your students.

Discuss with your partner regularly what the learning objectives are. We set aside time each week to determine what students need to learn next. Share grading and late-work policies so that you are both on the same page. Determine who evaluates certain assignments, and who calls certain parents when academic concerns arise. Determine how much of a teaching role and supporting role you each play. Will you teach fifty-fifty? Will one of you play the support role? Will you run small-group instruction and implement flexible grouping? Although it is important to make such decisions early in your relationship to avoid conflict or misunderstanding, keep in mind that roles and responsibilities change along with student needs and curriculum objectives. Flexibility throughout the year is the key.

Model for Determining Expectations

The following checklist and activities are meant to help guide partners new to co-teaching and open the door to honest and practical discussion about roles and responsibilities. Review with your co-teaching partner the model of establishing co-teaching expectations. Next, refer to the co-teaching discussion topics to individually guide each partner to complete the "mine" column in the blank form for establishing co-teaching expectations. When you come back together, discuss and record your partner's expectations in the "my partner" column. Finally, come to an agreement about the expectations for your shared students and classroom.

Exhibit 2-1
Establishing Co-Teaching Expectations
A Model

Expectation	Mine	My Partner's	Our Classroom
Classroom policies and procedures	• Bathroom during breaks, unless emergency • Sharpen pencil not OK during instruction or directions • Several students pass out papers; pass and collect papers without discussion • Help: three before me	• Bathroom OK except when lecturing • Have a can of sharpened pencils by the sharpener; students exchange broken one for sharpened one • Assign job roles to specific students • Three before me	• Bathroom during class breaks only, unless emergency • Can of sharpened pencils with predetermined amount each month • Assign job roles • Three before me: reread, ask neighbor one, ask neighbor two
Teaching styles and preferences	• Humor and flexibility during a lesson • Student-centered a goal, but find that I do too much teacher-centered • Student choice	• Flexibility in lesson plans based on student needs • Engage students in lessons whenever possible • Pair learning, not a lot of direct lecture	• Flexibility, humor in meeting student needs • Goal: more student-centered and student-involved instruction

Behavior management	• Try to be consistent • Gentle reminder before sending out of room for break or time in another room • Few detentions • Ignore whining or begging • Still struggle with getting students to work independently or productively in small groups	• Quiet, personal, specific warnings to student • Allow choice for a two-minute time away • Detention last resort • Engage students as much as possible • Positive praise, attention slips, positive behavior cards • Team belief, not dictator	• Consistency • Personal, specific, gentle reminder • Time away for student to regroup • Train students for independent work time, anchor activities • Positive praise, positive phone call home
Academic goals	• Diverse, rich, and challenging at individual levels • Perform at grade level independently	• Challenge every student at his or her level but continuously raise expectations • Provide opportunities for students to demonstrate what they know in various ways	• Challenge every student with diverse learning opportunities for continued growth

Classroom Management: An Activity for New Partners

Discuss with your co-teacher how each of you would respond to these scenarios. Keep in mind there are no right or wrong answers; these activities are a means to address realistic classroom situations. Use these three questions to guide your discussion for each scenario:

1. How would each teacher respond to this situation?
2. Would you respond differently if the student were GE or SE?
3. What happens with the rest of the class?

Exhibit 2-2
Co-Teaching Discussion Topics

Classroom policies and procedures

- Bathroom policy
- Pencil sharpening
- Drinks of water
- Use or answering of telephone
- Collecting and returning papers
- Asking for help when needed

Teaching Styles and Preferences

- Acceptable noise level in the room during:
  - Teacher lecture
  - Small group work
  - Independent work time
- Transition strategies:
  - Countdown (five to one)
  - Sound cue
  - Light cue
- Allotting time for student completion of work
  - Having enrichment work ready for students finishing early
  - Providing additional time for students who need it
  - Accepting partially completed assignments
- Interacting with students

Behavior Management

- What kind of positive behavior reinforcers?
- How do you handle vocal refusers?
- How do you handle passive refusers?
- How do you handle blurters?
- How do you handle wanderers and other off-taskers?

Academic Goals

- Professional and teaching goals for student achievement
- Quality of student assignments
- Time teaching and interacting with students in the GE classroom

Worksheet 2.1
Establishing Co-Teaching Expectations

Expectation	Mine	My Partner's	Our Classroom
Classroom policies/Procedures			
Teaching styles/Preferences			
Behavior Management			
Academic Goals			

Scenario A

(Setting: Ms. Grant, the GE teacher, is holding a small-group lesson at a table while Ms. Waterhouse, the SE teacher, is in another small-group lesson at a table across the room. The remainder of the class is working independently at their desks.) A student working independently at his desk suddenly gets frustrated, slams his book on the floor, and shouts, "This is stupid!"

Scenario B

(Setting: Mr. Nelson, the SE teacher, is conducting a whole-class math activity using the overhead. Ms. Matthews, the GE teacher, kneels next to a student's desk in the back of the room, helping her understand the math concept Mr. Nelson is demonstrating.) Throughout Mr. Nelson's lesson, a student persists in talking to the one seated in front of him about the upcoming dance. Mr. Nelson has already stopped his activity twice to tell the student to be quiet and now, the third time, has asked the student to step out into the hallway. The student yells, "What? I didn't do anything!"

Scenario C

(Setting: Students are working independently on a new assignment. Mrs. Adams, the GE teacher, and Mr. Shapiro, the SE teacher, are both circulating around the room, helping individual students as needed.) Mrs. Adams is working with an SE student who is clearly becoming increasingly agitated.

Sharing Responsibilities: Suggested Approaches

An easy way to begin working in the co-teaching model is to have the GE teacher lead a whole class lesson while the SE teacher circulates around the room, or vice versa. One teacher helps redirect students who are off-task and clarifies the main ideas of the lesson. She may stand next to a student who is not actively engaged in the lesson and subtly redirect him. (This approach is often referred to as proximity and is much easier to practice with more than one adult in a classroom of thirty-plus students.) Or she can kneel down next to a student who has an auditory processing deficit and ask him to tell her back in his own words the key concepts just discussed to ensure understanding. She can clarify or ask questions of the teacher who is instructing the whole class, with the purpose of reiterating key points.

Model A

In a seventh grade social studies classroom, Ms. Hartline is the GE teacher conducting an interactive slide-and-notes lecture on the Byzantine Empire, while her co-teaching partner Ms. Sheridan, an SE teacher, is circulating around the room. The class of thirty-four students takes notes while Ms. Hartline explains the slides. Ms. Sheridan stops first behind a student in the back of the room who is not actively engaged in the slide show. He is playing with a little plastic toy skateboard on his knee under his desk. Ms. Sheridan approaches him and puts her hand out, gesturing for the student to hand over the skateboard. The student puts the little toy in her hand. She then points to his blank page of notes and he begins to write.

Ms. Sheridan continues circulating around the room, ensuring that all students are engaged. She stops next to Billy, a student with an auditory processing deficit. She bends down next to his desk and quietly asks him who the leader was of the Byzantine Empire (a fact Ms. Hartline reviewed two minutes ago with the previous slide). Billy tells her the correct answer, and she asks if he has any questions about anything in the lecture. He shakes his head no. Ms. Sheridan continues circulating around the room.

As Ms. Hartline wraps up the last slide of the lesson, Ms. Sheridan asks aloud for the benefit of the rest of the students, "So, who was the leader that created a bunch of laws?"

Ms. Hartline responds, "Can anyone help us out with that question?"

A student raises her hand and responds, "Justinian."

"Who agrees and thinks it was Justinian?" Ms. Sheridan asks the class. Many hands go up. "You're right. And remember that name, because it is going to come up a little later too."

Another way to begin implementing the co-teaching model is through small-group work. The GE and SE teacher both may need to offer instruction in small groups. Your once-overcrowded and overwhelming class of thirty students becomes a much more manageable two or more groups of fifteen, ten, or even five. These groups can be differentiated by ability, interest, or random choice. The need for these groups would arise during planning time on the basis of some form of pre-assessment. There are a variety of configurations for small groups. The two most common are the class divided in half with one teacher instructing each group, where the groups can then switch after a predetermined amount of time; and groups working like the "centers" model, where there can be three to five groups of students with four to seven students in each group.

Model B

In a fourth grade language arts lesson, Ms. Miller, the GE teacher, has half the class with her in the front of the room, while Ms. Hawkins, the SE teacher, has the remaining students with her in the back of the room. Both groups are sitting in a circle with the teacher as part of the circle. The groupings are based on ability shown in a writing sample completed the previous day. Ms. Miller works with the remedial or lower group, while Ms. Hawkins teaches the higher-ability group. Ms. Hawkins shows a picture of a girl eating ice cream and asks the students to write five complete sentences describing the picture. Each sentence has to have at least two adjectives. She checks in with each student as they are writing their sentences.

Meanwhile, Ms. Miller shows a picture of a boy on a skateboard to her group. She asks the students to raise their hand and describe what they see in as much detail as they can. She writes the words down on her large dry-erase board. She then underlines the words and tells the students that these words are called adjectives. Again, this is a remedial lesson based on a preassessment, so this is not the first exposure to adjectives. Ms. Miller knows, however, that she must break down the concepts very simplistically to ensure that students grasp their meaning.

An obvious benefit of co-teaching is classroom management. Many veteran teachers have struggled with the challenges posed by reluctant learners. We were able to deal with such a situation as a team when Carrie joined our class.

Model C

Carrie came to us after having been shuffled to yet another family member in the area. Her cousin was the last one who would take her after Carrie had finally worn out her welcome at her grandmother's. She was a tough-talking, petite thirteen-year-old, sharp and witty, but also bitter and angry, prone to outbursts and tantrums. Her skills were low, but not shockingly so. After hearing her story, we committed ourselves to fostering a stable and positive environment for her. At first, she simply observed quietly. She took in how the other students behaved, and it seemed that we would all be successful. After just two days, however, the outbursts began.

"No!" Carrie shouted, refusing to read aloud and then looking around the room for reactions from the other kids. They looked at her in disbelief, and then at Maureen to see her reaction.

"You won't read, Carrie?" Maureen asked to clarify.

Cold stare. "No!" Carrie smirked and looked around again for approval.

And so the daily challenges began. When Maureen was solo with the class, any chance at learning was completely derailed. During projects, Carrie would sabotage group effort at success. Quiet corner discussion meant to help her refocus resulted in Carrie raising her voice or shutting down entirely, while the rest of the class tried their best to keep working. She still continued to refuse to read aloud—even though we knew she could read quite well. Simply put, this one student was completely destroying the climate we had all worked so hard to create.

Something was different, however, during the periods when Mindy was in the room. If Carrie began to melt down, Mindy was able to take her out to walk and talk while Maureen kept the rest of the class on task. Maureen knew that Mindy shared her expectations for how Carrie should behave and that she would support whatever disciplinary consequence Maureen felt was appropriate. Mindy was able to reiterate to Carrie one-on-one why she was expected to practice reading aloud or participate in a group project, while Carrie could blow off steam outside. Maureen was also able to elicit from Carrie ideas for what might help her stay on task and benefit from being in class, and together with Maureen they could determine how to make it work for everyone. Carrie got the added attention she needed; she learned about problem solving, and the rest of the class could continue learning.

We discovered that Carrie, who had so little control in her life, craved control at school. When we offered her a choice to complete a project alone or with a group, she opted for working alone outside of the class, and one of us could check her progress periodically. Eventually, Carrie began to complete her work. She also began to participate more appropriately in whole-class discussion. Carrie felt, for a time, successful. Whenever Maureen sensed an impending explosion, Mindy would again take her out of the room for a walk and conference. Had it not been for the fact that there were two of us available, the needs of thirty students would have been sacrificed for the sake of just one.

Carrie's story illustrates many benefits of co-teaching, not the least of which is that thirty-plus students can continue to be engaged despite the distraction caused by just one other student. The ability to group or pull one student—or more—away from the rest of the group greatly alleviates the stress that both teachers and students endure in today's overcrowded classrooms.

Without a partner, teachers must deal with such situations alone. Too often, in our isolation, we educators begin to question whether we are doing the right thing. Did we say something wrong? Could we have done that differently to avoid the situation? How can we . . . ? With a partner who knows the dynamics of the class and our teaching style, problem solving becomes a natural part of teaming.

Flexibility

As with teaching in general, flexibility in the co-teaching classroom is vital. Partnering with a colleague requires both parties to be aware the differences in teaching style, and to respect the unique abilities of the other teacher. In the same sense, we are teaching our students to be aware and respectful of the differences among all of us as learners. We address their needs in many ways throughout the day: one-on-one or small-group for ability-based skills instruction in spelling; choice pairs that are based on learning preferences; small groups for differing ability-based skills in math; whole-group instruction when introducing a new concept or skill to the entire class. In other words, change is a constant, and flexibility allows change to happen so regularly that students don't think it unusual in the least. It becomes easy for you and for them to adjust.

Planning

We find that planning with a colleague makes teaching a truly joyful profession. As co-teachers, we design assessments and lessons together, teach together, and laugh together. In fact, our co-teaching experiences have been so successful that the energy and rejuvenation spread throughout the entire staff, and common planning time with curriculum and grade level teams is now the norm. We cannot imagine returning to the isolation of the past in the traditional system. In planning together, we also get to know all of our students better, as we can brainstorm and discuss specific challenges and possible strategies for meeting unique academic or behavioral needs. Our teaching and our students' learning have benefited from teaching in a collaborative, and much more creative, setting. Thanks to the support we have received, we are able to sustain the positive energy that regular collaborative planning time allows.

Coordinated Scheduling

Following the initial success of the pilot program at McKinleyville Middle School, the pilot team decided that other teachers should give it a try. Fortunately, staff were excited about the results of Mindy and Julie's program. Many teachers were willing to try integration, even knowing it would require some extra time and creative energy. Given the number of IEPs and the two SE teachers on site, the pilot team decided that the next step would be to incorporate the program into the three seventh grade core classes and one sixth grade core class. (Resource students were already integrated into science and math.) The plan: Mindy would keep working with Julie in eighth grade core and would integrate her sixth grade IEP caseload into Jennifer Adams's sixth grade core class. In seventh grade, SE teacher Holly Matthews's caseload of students with IEPs would be distributed evenly among the three classes. Holly would work with the three teachers in their two core classes for two periods (one per core) each day, supporting students and co-teaching when appropriate, or (to the degree the two teachers) were comfortable.

It seemed manageable at the outset, but as time went by, Holly was so busy running from core class to core class, trying to keep up with what was going on in each room, that we had little time for collaborating and even less for co-teaching. Although Holly led some whole-class lessons, the first year we worked mostly on differentiating the curriculum during our once-a-week planning periods.

If we were to do it over, we would integrate Holly's entire caseload into one core (if numbers allowed). If the numbers required that students be integrated into more than one GE core, we would schedule planning times for all three teachers. We would request release time, once per trimester, for long-term planning purposes.

We learned that it makes much more sense to integrate our SE students (and teachers) into as few classes as possible. This way students would benefit from clustering, as our gifted and talented students did, and teachers could focus on what went on in fewer classes, therefore better supporting both teachers and students. Full integration now involves targeted core classes, one or two math classes, and one or two science classes at each grade level. This is a much more manageable system for the SE teachers. Exhibits 2.3 and 2.4 demonstrate our current SE teacher daily schedules and master schedule.

Administrative Support for Teachers

Just as a coach functions to facilitate an effective team, so must the administrators of a school or district be actively engaged in facilitating change. In our ever-changing educational climate, the administrator must be a creative thinker, working outside the box in considering options for staffing, resources and professional development. Most important, as we face diminishing budgets and a rising emphasis on meeting standards, administrators and teachers must recognize that making collaboration and co-teaching happen does not necessarily mean that more money is needed. On the contrary, staff members need to determine priorities, dedicate energy, and *redistribute* resources to support those priorities. For us, the priority is that all students will succeed at grade level and be challenged to grow beyond that, all through a collaborative approach. Administrative support is so essential to success in any attempts to co-teach or integrate SE and GE classes that we devote Chapter 4 to this subject.

Exhibit 2-3
McKinleyville Middle School

Master Schedule 2006-07
2/2/2007

Teacher	1	2	3	4	5	6	7	8
				Lunch Block				
Adams	Core 8	Core 8	Core 8	Lunch	Print	Tech	Prep	Print
Gianinni-Previde	Core 8	Core 8	Core 8	Lunch	Core 8 R	Core 8 R	Prep	Core 8 R
Nelson	Core 8	Core 8	Core 8	Lunch	Core 8	Core 8	Prep	Core 8
Grant	Alg 1A	Alg 1	Prep	Lunch	Alg 1	Alg 1	Alg 1A	Foundations
Hoffman	Prep	Sci 8 R		Lunch	Sci 8		Sci 8	Intervention M
Taylor	Core 7	Acad. Support	Acad. Support	Lunch	Core 7 R	Prep	Core 7 R	Core 7 R
Pilarowski	Core 7	Core 7	Core 7	Lunch	Core 7	Prep	Core 7	Core 7
Waterhouse	Core 7	Core 7	Core 7	Lunch	Intervention R	Prep	Intervention R	Intervention Prep
Sheridan	Foundations	Foundations	Prep	Lunch	Prep Math	Prep Math	Tech	Foundations
Himango	Prep	Sci 7	Sci 7	Lunch	Sci 7	Sci 7	Sci 7	Sci 8
Klar	Success	Prep	Success	Core 6	Lunch	Core 6	Core 6	Success
Howe	Core 6 R	Prep	Core 6 R SS	Core R LA	Lunch	Core 6R	Core 6R	Core 6R
Deason	Core 6	Prep	Core 6 SS	Core 6 LA	Lunch	Core 6	Core 6	Core 6
McGuire	Math 6	Math 6	Prep	Math 6*	Lunch	Success	Math 6*	Math 6
Kamprath	Prep	Sci 6	Sci 8	Sci 6	Lunch	Sci 6	Sci 6	Sci 6
Weiderman		PE 6 A/B		Lunch	Prep	Fine Arts	Fine Arts	Fine Arts
Hozven		Prep	Span Elect	Span Core sup	Lunch	Span 1A		
Ross	Adv Band	Beg Band						
Hall	PE 7/8	PE 7/8	PE 7/8	Lunch	Prep	PE 7/8	PE 7/8	PE 7/8
Esparza	PE 6/7	PE 6 A/B	PE 6/7	Lunch	Prep	PE 6/7	PE 6/7	PE 6/7
Fattig	Intervention R	Prep	Intervention R	Core 6 R	Lunch	Core 6 R	Core 7 R	
Matthews		Intervention M	Acad Support		Core 8 R	Prep Math	Acad Support	
Shapiro	SDC	SDC	SDC	Lunch	SDC	SDC	Prep	6th BSS support
Culps	OC	OC	OC	Lunch	OC	Prep	OC	OC

Course* = Paced Course   Algebra 1A = First of a 2 year Algebra Course
Foundations = Foundations in Algebra   Algebra 1 = First year Algebra Course

Exhibit 2-4
Daily Schedules

Special Education Teachers
Daily Schedule
Fattig Schedule 2006–07

	Period 1	Per. 2	Per. 3	Per. 4	Per. 5	Per. 6	Per. 7	Per. 8
Mon	IV Prep	Acad supp	Acad supp	Lunch	SPED prep	IV 7 prep	Acad supp	Core 7*
Tues	IV R 8	Acad supp	IV R 7	Lunch	IV R 7	Core 6*	Core 7*	IV R 8
Wed	IV R 8	Acad supp	IV R 7	Lunch	IV R 7	Core 6*	Core 7*	IV R 8
Thur	IV R 8	Howe prep	IV R 7	Lunch	IV R 7	Core 6*	IV 8 prep	IV R 8
Fri	MUSD	MUSD	MUSD	MUSD	MUSD	MUSD	MUSD	MUSD

IV R 7 = response to intervention 7th grade reading class
IV R 8 = response to intervention 8th grade reading class
MUSD = McKinleyville Union School District program specialist
Prep = planning period with GE teacher
Matthews schedule 2006–07
(.74 FTE)

	Period 1	Per. 2	Per. 3	Per. 4	Per. 5	Per. 6	Per. 7	Per. 8
Tues	Alg 1a	Sci 8*	Acad supp	Lunch	Core 8*	Prep math	Acad supp	Core 8*
Wed	_____	_____	Math prep	Lunch	Core 8*	Culps prep	Acad supp	Core 8*
Thur	Alg 1a	Acad supp	Acad supp	Lunch	Core 8*	Prep math	Acad supp	Prep
Fri	Alg 1a	Acad supp	Acad supp	Lunch	Prep math	Prep math	Acad supp	Prep

Exit Card

Exit cards are a form of informal assessment that allows students to reflect on new learning or anticipate learning yet to come. For the teacher, the purpose can be to reinforce new learning, assess students' prior knowledge on key concepts or terms, and supply information about how to plan for the following day. We offer exit card prompts orally or in writing, but we have found that we must keep them short so that students can complete them thoroughly and therefore be truly effective. A completed exit card is a student's "ticket" out of class that day or period.

At the end of Parts One and Two of this book, we present sample exit cards for you to experience in our effort to support you in reflecting on your own teaching and learning. Our student exit cards are usually brief enough for every student to complete one within five to seven minutes, but we employ more thought-provoking prompts for you here. Although we typically give students exit card prompts on the overhead projector while they respond on index cards, you may simply journal your responses in whatever format you prefer. (See more on exit cards in Chapter Four.)

1. Who is someone you can begin collaborating with tomorrow?
2. What obstacles do your staff members need to overcome to make collaboration a reality throughout your site?
3. What steps could you take to move toward a co-teaching model?

Part Two

Working in the Differentiated Classroom

Chapter Three

Differentiation Essentials

Developing academically responsive classrooms is important for a country built on the twin values of equity and excellence. Our schools can achieve both of these competing values only to the degree that they can establish heterogeneous communities of learning (attending to issues of equity) built solidly on high-quality curriculum and instruction that strive to maximize the capacity of each learner (attending to issues of excellence).

Carol Ann Tomlinson (1999)

Traditionally, the term *differentiation* has been reserved for discussion of modifying curriculum to better meet the needs of *gifted* children. Sometimes these students are our greatest joy; they complete work meticulously and find learning about anything exciting. Other times they are the ones who get it so easily that they become bored in school and disengage from learning activities if not adequately challenged. Because such students consider school a joke, they may act out, space out, or not complete assignments. Educators therefore try to help these students find areas of interest, hoping for something that might create a spark. We take them deeper into the curriculum, trying to challenge them and inspire them to want to learn simply for the sake of learning. It is hard to do.

What is Differentiation?

In the summer of 2000, our district gifted and talented program (GATE) coordinator, Nancy Wheeler, implemented summer professional development training on differentiation to meet the needs of gifted children. Coincidentally, that same year Mindy Fattig, McKinleyville Middle School's resource specialist, piloted the integration program at our school. From that point on, we applied a much broader meaning of the term *differentiation*. We use it now to refer to adaptation of all curriculum to better meet the needs not just of gifted kids but of all kids.

It was, after all, Mindy's goal that her special education students receive instruction in the general education classes, thus allowing them full-time access to the standards curriculum. These kids would be held accountable for knowing the standards just as every other child in the general education classroom would. We had to be creative in helping these kids access the standards curriculum. The simple answer was to differentiate.

We define *differentiation* as reflective and responsive teaching, based on the understanding that every classroom is composed of a variety of learning styles and abilities. We must credit our gurus on the topic for helping us develop our own definition of what differentiation is: Nancy Craig, the Sacramento City Schools GATE coordinator; Carol Ann Tomlinson; Susan Winebrenner; Jay McTighe; and Grant Wiggins, as well as our very own Nancy Wheeler. Wiggins and McTighe describe differentiation as "a strategy, never done, always ongoing, a philosophy that guides our teaching and student learning" (1998, p. 13).

What it is Not

However you define it, differentiation is *not* individualizing every assignment for every child, every day. Far from it! There will be days on which, on the basis of your reflective and responsive teaching, you determine that whole-class instruction is what every child needs. Sometimes you simply have to break a class into two groups: one that needs a quick review of fundamentals with your support, and a second group that is ready to go on to the practice work independently. You have likely decided at this point that you already differentiate every single day in your classroom. Exhibits 3.1 and 3.2 list the critical components of differentiation as well as the basic practices in a differentiated classroom.

Knowing the Students

Knowing our students and what they need if they are to be successful is certainly a key to being an effective educator. When we first went to an integrated program, we tried to be sensitive to the fact that students can be cruel and tease each other. Students from Mindy's pull-out program suffered from low self-esteem, sadly labeling themselves as "dummies" and "retards." Unfortunately, some of the general education kids reinforced the stigma through their attitude and unkind comments. Therefore, building self-esteem for all students was a high priority

Exhibit 3-1
Critical Components of Differentiation

- Establishing a common vocabulary within your classroom and ultimately throughout your school
- Getting to know your students'
  - Abilities (cum folders and portfolios; state tests, meetings, etc.)
  - Interests
  - Learning styles
- Community building throughout the year
  - Establishing what is fair as opposed to what each person needs
  - Giving students opportunities to get to know their own and each other's learning strengths, styles, and needs
  - Practicing strategies and support for community building
- Assessing Students Regularly
  - Formally
    - End-of-unit tests
    - Essays
    - State assessments
  - Informally
    - Pretests
    - Exit cards
    - Roaming checklists
    - Informal writing prompts and review questions
    - Short quizzes
    - KWHL (What do students know? What do they want to know? How will they learn it? What did they learn?)
    - Student surveys (thumbs up or down, discussion, etc.)
- Using instructional strategies to meet diverse student needs
  - Flexible grouping
  - Bloom's taxonomy: levels of critical thinking
  - Asking differentiated questions
  - Tiered assignments
  - Menus and contracts: allow choice and independent learning

Exhibit 3-2
Fundamental Practices in an Effective Differentiated Classroom

FLEXIBILITY of

- Teaching modes
- Learning styles
- Assessment
- Grouping

ONGOING ASSESSMENT

- Formal
- Informal

GROUPING by

- Readiness
- Interest
- Learning style
- Whole class
- Individual
- Pairs
- Small group

APPROPRIATE CHALLENGE

- Interesting and engaging learning tasks
- Taking student from where he or she is to where he or she needs to be

STUDENT-TEACHER COLLABORATION

- Student consciously providing information about his or her learning
- Student making responsible choices
- Teachers assessing, conferencing, and adjusting accordingly

Adapted from *Leadership for Differentiating Schools and Classrooms* by Tomlinson and Allan (2000).

for us, and we had to do some serious up-front training. Of course, community building is important in all classroom settings, but we have found that in a newly integrated classroom it is crucial to fostering a kind learning environment—early and throughout the year.

The differentiated classroom must operate on two very important principles:

1. All students are at varying levels of readiness in all topics. We each bring unique experiences and talents to the classroom.

2. These differences are embraced and celebrated in our classroom. Students should gain knowledge of their strengths and weakness as a blueprint for how they learn and where they need assistance.

In a truly differentiated classroom, students are working on a variety of assignments at a given time. We don't want them to compare their assignments, to feel that one is harder or easier than another, but rather to accept an assignment as what each student needs at a particular time. Even though integration of special education students is no longer new at our school, we continue to practice explicit community- and character-building activities schoolwide, ensuring a sense of safety and acceptance for all students, in the classrooms and on the playground.

In this section, we share some examples of fun and easy ways for students and teachers to get to know each other, socially and academically, thus creating a warm and supportive learning environment:

- Welcome letters
- Success or achieve-and-aspire graphs
- Multiple intellingences and get-to-know mobile Bingo
- Crush the can or cracker
- Interest inventories

Welcome Letters

We greet each student at the door daily with a smile and a handshake. On the first day of school, the child also receives a personal letter from each of us that welcomes him to the class and tells him a bit about us, our hobbies and family, and our summer. The first assignment is for the student to write a reply, telling us about her hobbies, family, summer vacation, likes, dislikes, or just anything she thinks might be helpful for us to know. These letters come in handy all year long. Not only do we learn a bit about the students' personal lives but we also learn about their writing skills and academic concerns. We have even used these letters in creating get-to-know Bingo (Exhibit 3.7, later in this chapter) to play during the first week.

Success Graphs

A success graph is just one way we achieve multiple beginning-of-the-year goals. We help students accept their own and others' strengths and areas of weakness by designing a success graph. The form can certainly vary from grade to grade, especially if the entire school is planning to use them. Our sixth graders create "achieve and aspire" graphs, while eighth graders make "success graphs." (See the lesson plan that follows.) Whatever we choose to call our graph, we begin with teacher talk, modeling our own strengths and weaknesses. (We try as often as possible to refer to deficits as "areas to improve"; we want our kids to understand that there is always room for growth.)

When we teach together, Mindy tells the class, "I'm really good at writing, but I'm a lousy artist. I've always struggled with drawing and art, but my daughter loves it and really excels at it. I ask her to help me draw." Maureen adds, "Mindy can read superfast, but I read slowly, and I get frustrated sometimes in workshops when they don't give me enough time to read an article."

Maureen tells the class, "I have an amazing sense of direction when I need to direct my husband Bruce somewhere, but when he is inland, he cannot find north, south, east, or west. On the other hand, he can remember every detail about every beach cove along the West Coast, where they are, and what their names are. To me, they all look beautiful, but they also mostly look the same, and I could not for the life of me remember all of their names and locations."

This modeling leads to a whole-class discussion of various personal and academic strengths and areas that may need improvement. We then create a graph with a vertical line showing degree of mastery (Exhibits 3.3 and 3.4). If you are super good at something,

Exhibit 3-3
Student "Achieve and Aspire" Graphs

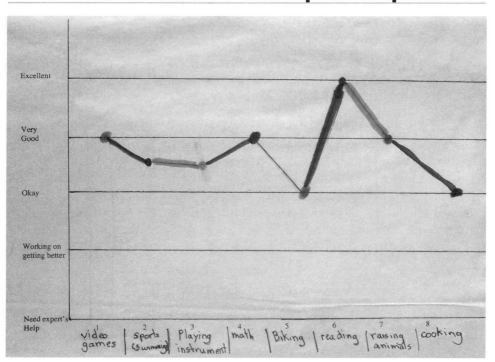

Exhibit 3-4
Student "Achieve and Aspire" Graphs

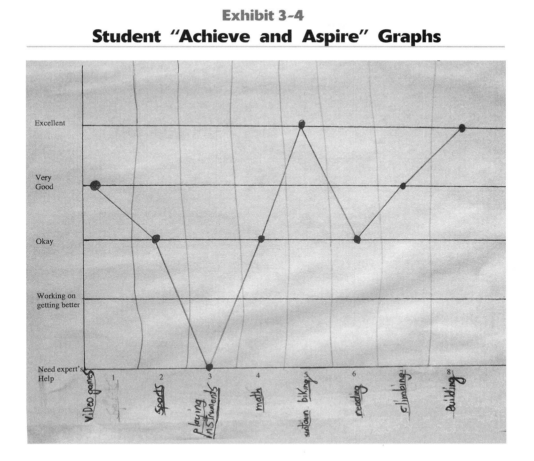

you might be considered an "expert" at that skill. The other extreme might be "needs the support of an expert" or "in training." Your class can decide how many degrees to include, and what to call them. We then list the various skills, both personal and academic, along the horizontal line. We have found it best to leave some blank spots for the kids that might not find themselves to be at the expert level in any of the skills listed by the class; everyone has some skill at which he or she excels, and we encourage students to be sure to include that.

Consider variations on the success graph that are based purely on academic skills or personal hobbies. Either way, you will learn a lot about your students, and the discussion is a valuable one you can refer back to throughout the year.

Furthermore, we can use this activity as a jump-off spot for a minilesson on how we all have our own strengths and weaknesses and therefore different academic needs. We all need help with some skills, and it is OK to ask for help when you need it. To illustrate this point, Mindy says, "Look, if I have a broken arm (a temporary weakness), would I want my doctor to give me the same kind of treatment he gives Sam with her headache? What kind of doctor would I be if I even tried to give the same treatment to such different ailments? In the same way, why would I, the teacher, provide stick-drawing drill and practice to an accomplished artist like Joe here? I am the one who needs help drawing stick figures. Joe is ready to be introduced to 'perspective' drawing, and I owe it to him to provide the tools to help him learn it."

The templates in exhibit 3.5 are for your use or modification.

Exhibit 3-5
____ 's Achieve and Aspire Graph

	Math	Cooking	Baseball	Public speaking	Playing instrument	Art	Reading	Soccer	Computers	
My personal best (EXPERT)										
I feel good about this										
I need some help (from experts)										

Sixth Grade Template.

Success Graph Lesson Plan
(Julie Giannini-Previde, Eighth Grade Core, McKinleyville Middle School)

Objectives:

- Students gain understanding of the strengths and weaknesses of their classmates and teachers.
- Students gain greater understanding of class philosophy.
- Students create a graph.

Materials:

- Paper, writing utensil.
- Large construction paper, art supplies.
- Optional: photographs of each student.

Instruction:

- As a class, students come up with a list of skills people have, such as cooking, playing an instrument, a sport. Students copy list onto their paper.
- When the list is complete (ten to twenty skills), students rank their skill level for each activity on a scale of 1 to 10.
- I send the paper home and as homework students add five skills of their own to the list. This is so kids who didn't rank themselves a 9 or 10 on the class list can identify their own stellar skills.
- The next day, students create a graph with their data. Decorate and add photos.
- Once they are posted, discuss the fact that no one is good at everything, but no one is bad at everything either. Every single member of the class has great variation in ability level.

Follow-Up:

- This is the perfect time to read Reavis' *The Animal School*.
- I follow this activity with an autobiographical essay to relate a success or failure and how students have grown as a result.

Multiple Intelligences or Get-to-Know Mobile Bingo

Mobile Bingo is a fun get-to-know activity that addresses actual student hobbies, vacations, families, and learning preferences and styles. Kids wander around the room introducing themselves and learning about each other, collecting signatures in the process. If you teach your students about Howard Gardner's multiple intelligences (we recommend you do), you can design a Bingo game based on his book of the same name (1997). An alternative version of the game can focus on what your students tell you about themselves in their welcome letters (if they read a lot over the summer, played football or video games, and so on). You can then follow up with a lesson on multiple intelligences and have students group themselves by learning style or preference. They are likely to find they have more in common with someone than they ever thought possible. Samples from one of Maureen's classes follow.

Exhibit 3-6
Multiple Intelligences Mobile BINGO

DIRECTIONS: Roam and find people who fit the descriptions. Introduce yourself if you do not remember someone's name. Write the person's name neatly over the boxed description with which he or she identifies. You must write a name only once, and you must complete two solid lines before calling "BINGO!"

Would like to be the master of ceremonies at the talent show this year	Draws graphs or pictures to help learn math problems	Learns best working alone	Takes apart pens and pencils during class	Prefers being around people instead of being alone
Can knit and sew	Enjoys tide-pooling	Sings, hums, or whistles often	Would have had trouble following directions to this game if they were given only orally	Hobbies are mostly done alone
Computes math problems quickly	Plays the trumpet or piano	GIMME	Creates images and pictures in head	Enjoys diaries, journals, silent reading
Is good at jigsaw puzzles and mazes	Learns best when working with others	Is good at pattern games such as chess and checkers	Volunteers for outdoor cleanup projects	Cringes when music is off key
Prefers observing outdoors over people-watching	Is a good listener, negotiator, and persuader	Likes discussion, debate, and speeches	Learns best by moving around, acting things out	Can describe own strengths and weaknesses

Based on Howard Gardner's *Multiple Intelligences* and Teacher's Curriculum Institute.

Interest Inventories

Another way to get to know your students and their interests for lesson design is to administer an interest inventory early in the year. Examples are available on the Internet. One we use in modified form is an extensive inventory from Diane Heacox's *Differentiating Instruction in the Regular Classroom* (2002). We keep these inventories on file for reference when designing projects and choose-to-do activities. In addition, we recommend your reviewing the students' cum files and previous assessment scores in getting to know your students.

Crush the Can or Cracker We use this activity, adapted from Robi Kronberg, early in the school year to demonstrate how hurtful words can be. Again, because students can tend to be judgmental and even careless with their comments, we feel that this physical activity has long-lasting impact that we can refer back to throughout the school year.

Exhibit 3-7
Get-to-Know Mobile BINGO

DIRECTIONS: Roam and find people who fit the descriptions. Introduce yourself if you do not remember someone's name. Write the person's name neatly over the box with the description with which he or she identifies. You must write a name only once, and you must complete two solid lines before calling BINGO!

Spends time in Vermont every summer with family	Works on cars with grandpa and plays football	Swam and skateboarded at aunt and uncle's this summer	Watched Chicago Cubs play at Wrigley Field this summer	Went to Washington this summer, swims, hunts, likes meeting people
Has a pet frog that shares a name with MMS teacher	Rode the Royal Flush at Las Vegas water park this summer	Has four cats, five fish, and two hermit crabs as pets	Plays Rise of Nations, football, and baseball, and is from Long Beach, CA	Went to Vans Skate Park and Marine World
Spent summer in Pennsylvania and saw the Phillies play	Collects four-leaf clovers	Petted a baby black bear in Oregon this summer	Loves animals and having fun, and plans to be a lawyer	Will have a new baby brother in four months
Took new family boat to Lake Almanor this summer	Had pink hair this summer	Has earned a white belt, green stripe in karate and loves sushi	Draws dragons and knights, Leonin, and Doku	Just got a birthday hamster

Crush the Can Lesson Plan

(Adapted from Robi Kronberg)

In this activity, students identify hurtful comments and then feel and show others how those words affect them personally. We suggest using soda or juice cans for older kids, and crackers for younger kids. We keep crushed cans on display throughout the school year, either hanging from the ceiling or stacked. This provides a visual reminder to the students that words can have a permanent impact. You can also follow up with "buildups"—comments to make people feel better—and keep this list on display for the entire school year.

Objectives:

- Students develop understanding of the negative power of put-downs.
- Students gain greater understanding of class philosophy.

Materials:

- Something to crush that cannot be restored to its original state (soda can, juice can, crackers, toothpaste tube, toothpicks).
- Post-it notes (each student receives one to fifteen notes).

Instructions:

- Students are given a can of juice or soda (crackers in sandwich bags for younger kids, tube of toothpaste and toothpicks for older kids in small groups) and a stack of Post-its. While they drink their juice, they are instructed to write a put-down on each Post-it. (This should be a silent time of reflection so kids take it seriously. You may also want to remind them to keep it school-appropriate.)
- When they have finished juice and put-downs, prepare for a whole-group discussion.
- Students share put-downs while the rest of the class squeeze or crush juice or crackers to the extent that the put-down would hurt them. (Squeeze toothpaste onto a plate.) Depending on the maturity level of your group, it may be taken more seriously if the teachers collect the insults and read them aloud to the class.
- After going through all the put-downs, ask students now to restore their can or cracker or tube to its original condition (which they can't do).
- Discuss how put-downs crush or deplete people and our ability to restore our own self-esteem.

Follow-Up:

- Put crushed cans on display, accompanied by a slogan: "When you get a laugh at someone else's expense, it costs too much!"
- Create and post a list of buildups to counter the put-downs.

Section Summary   Getting to know your students and building a sense of community is vital to the success of any differentiated classroom, for many reasons:

- Understanding the positive and negative experiences students have had with previous learning
- Understanding students' strengths and preferred learning activities
- Understanding students' learning modalities and intelligences

Exhibit 3-8
Student Feedback on Crush the Can Activity

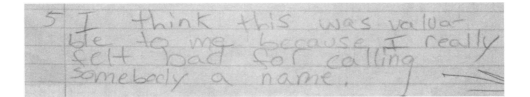

> This activity made me more aware not to make fun of people. I think that you should do this with next years 7th grades because I know some people who have been bullied and some bullies. I learned not make fun of people. I know what it's like and I don't want to give that pan to anyone else.

> 5 I think this was valuable to me because I really felt bad for calling somebody a name.

- Understanding students' interests and passions
- Helping students understand how they learn best and what they may need to work on for the year
- Helping students understand and respect the differences between people
- Helping students respect others and treat each other with compassion and kindness (Exhibits 3.8)

Developing Student Profiles

Once we feel we know our students well enough, we can develop student profiles, a helpful way to keep track of who needs what. The range of learners in every classroom is extensive, to say the least. But by examining the common learning styles, strengths, and weaknesses of students, we can identify representatives of the various learning groups we might work with every day.

Students might be categorized as "foundational" or "below grade level" (* or BGL), which for us means that the student functions at a level often below his or her grade and typically needs extra support with scaffolding or reteaching. Another category for classifying students is simply "grade level" (GL), indicating that the child performs relatively well on most grade-level tasks. "Advanced grade level" (AGL) students have shown that they are very bright and capable of high-level critical thinking in performing most tasks. Students may also carry with them the official labels of IEP or gifted. It did not take long during our early days of piloting an integrated class to discover that, even though a child is identified as special education, he or she is likely to have specific academic gifts as well. These are our "twice gifted" kids, and they too are in every classroom we have visited.

Of course, you need to get to know all of your students as individuals. We have frequently shared *The Animal School* in professional development workshops to illustrate the point that traditional public schools fail to recognize, address, and celebrate the differences among students. But our method of classification, inspired by Nancy Craig, might help you simplify the task of differentiating curriculum to meet everyone's needs. The students, of course, are not aware of these categories because of flexible grouping (see the subsection in Chapter Four).

Here is a list of students representing the broad spectrum of particular learning styles and needs in Any Classroom, U.S.A. Do you recognize similar traits among your students? Can you think of students who are not represented here that you might add? Use the spaces provided to note the students in your classes who come to mind as you read each description.

Jack (* or IEP): a concrete learner who needs visual representation to learn and demonstrate understanding of content material. He has a limited view of greater world issues. He struggles with grade-level reading and writing, and with transference of information. At lower levels, this student may have trouble with manipulatives.

_____

_____

Samantha (GL or IEP): has exceptional concept mastery in auditory terms but struggles with written language (and, at lower grades, with manipulatives).

_____

_____

Brian (underachieving gifted or AGL): demonstrates exceptional ability in reading, writing, and math, but only under certain circumstances. Typically a strong artist (drawing, music, acting, and so on).

_____

_____

Christy (GL): a grade-level learner who can adapt to auditory, visual, and spatial instruction and can use any or all of them with relative ease to demonstrate understanding. She has a fairly well-rounded knowledge base of the greater world and reads and writes at grade level with ease. She can easily manipulate most objects.

_____

_____

Anna (AGL): an exceptionally gifted and versatile learner. She is a perfectionist and has a wealth of knowledge about people and cultures from many backgrounds through time and place. Her reading and writing skills are superior.

_____

_____

Creating a classroom community where students recognize and accept our differences as being OK, and even worth celebrating, is especially important during the adolescent and young adult years. We have learned through experience that students need specific instruction and activities, in a nurturing setting, that raise awareness of strengths, weaknesses, and the ability to grow. In such an environment, we build trust and understanding. It is, of course, the teacher's responsibility to know her student's academic abilities, but it is crucial for teachers to connect to and truly know the whole student if differentiation, and consequently maximum student learning potential, is really going to be achieved.

Chapter Four

Planning Differentiated Lessons

Essential Steps

The first step in making differentiation work is the hardest. In fact, the same first step is required to make all teaching and learning effective: we have to know where we want to end up before we start out—and plan to get there.

Tomlinson (1999)

When planning a differentiated lesson, we consider the required course content, student skills, and resources that will promote learning. At first this process may seem overwhelming. It is well worth the extra time and effort, and remember to access colleagues as your best resource for support. Over time, you will be able to share common content area or grade-level lessons. Here is a list of steps we follow:

1. *Determine grade-level standard.* Establish what your students need to know in order to become proficient in a particular grade-level, content area standard. They are

likely to come to you with a variety of needs, so begin with the required grade-level standards.

2. *Determine topic of study.* Within the content area, what is the current topic of study: genetics and diseases, adding fractions, history of the Aztecs?

3. *Determine method of preassessment* so you can know where your students are and how they progress over the course of the study. Consider what skills and prior knowledge students need in order to show proficiency, and design a form of assessment to determine how you will plan instruction to meet student needs.

4. *Create three groups of students* (foundational, grade level, advanced grade level). ÑSUse the preassessment to group kids: Who is ready to work at grade level (GL), who needs scaffolding (*), and who needs more in-depth and complex learning to ensure engagement (AGL)?

5. *Determine target skills at each level using Bloom's taxonomy as a guide.* A review of Bloom's taxonomy as an integral part of differentiation follows (on page 50). The skills listed can be applied to a spectrum of learning levels.

6. *Develop critical questions that incorporate the target skills.* This step helps us as teachers think explicitly about what we want our students to be able to do and learn. We are basically turning the target skills (step five) into actions we can literally see students make over the course of the lesson.

7. *Decide if you want to use a tiered, menu, or linear contract* for teaching and learning. Several types of lesson plan samples and templates illustrate a variety of approaches to differentiated curriculum design.

8. *Reflect and respond.* Postassessment of student products may be used as new assessment for where to go next.

A *final product* is meant to show how well students have learned new information. A final product might be a test, an essay, an exit card, a report, and so on. Whether or not it is graded, we consider this postlesson assessment a means for helping the teacher determine what students need to learn (or relearn) next.

Now that you have determined your grade-level standard (step number one) and your topic of study (step number two), decide on your method of assessment.

Assessment to Drive Planning

There's no doubt about it: assessment is a tricky topic. In virtually every workshop we have presented, assessment and grading come up as the greatest concerns among educators. Differentiating curriculum has forced us to think about what exactly assessment means and more critically examine our grading philosophies—something we realized we had never done well, or responsibly. We address the issue of assessment as "grading" at the end of Part Two.

To us, assessment is a means for determining what a student needs to learn next. In the differentiated classroom, assessment is an ongoing practice and is not always graded. It is a tool for determining where your students are in their individual learning, and more important it serves as a starting point for your instructional planning.

Assessment Tools

An assessment could be as formal as a unit test or as informal as an exit card (seen at the end of Part One of this book and discussed further in this chapter). You can determine what a student needs to learn from a basic in-class assignment or from homework. We can decide from any of these tools whether Steven needs to practice basic fractions more before he moves on to decimal conversion. We can determine by simply talking to Joe about his independent reading if he comprehends the text he has chosen, and whether or not he needs to read at another level. By taking a class survey (thumbs up, to the side, or down), we can determine which groups are ready to delve deeper into content, which need to keep practicing the current subject, and which require more scaffolding to get the basic standard under their belts. We use assessments every day to help us make decisions about student learning, and we must teach to their needs.

Scenario

Students in Ms. Jackson's high school biology class were asked to identify on a diagram all the parts of a cell that they knew, as a measure of preassessment and a tool for planning her upcoming unit on animal cells. Reflecting on the assessments, Jackson determined that approximately 40 percent of her students could label successfully 90 percent or more of the parts, while 30 percent labeled very little or nothing and the rest of the class were successful in varying degrees. Using this information, she classified the students into the three learning groups:

1. Foundational: correctly identified and labeled less than 40 percent of parts correctly
2. Grade level: correctly identified and labeled 40–85 percent of parts correctly
3. Advanced grade level: correctly identified and labeled 85 percent or more of parts correctly

She then used this information to:

- Determine the entry level of each student
- Erase any guesswork or assumptions on her part of what the students know
- Plan upcoming unit (tiered assignment, contract, grouping students, peer lab partners, or even whole-class instruction)

Examples of Informal Assessment Tools

- Spelling pretests
- Exit cards
- Roaming checklists
- Informal writing prompts and review questions
- Short quizzes
- Student surveys

○ Discussion (thumbs up, thumbs down)

○ Written

• KWHL (What do students *know*? What do they *want* to know? *How* will they learn it? What did they *learn*?)

Spelling Pretests   To determine student needs regarding an upcoming spelling unit skill, teachers administer a whole-class oral or written spelling test, the results of which will determine the students' differentiated lessons for practice before the final assessment. These pretests are meant only to drive lesson planning and are not graded.

Exit Cards

Purpose:

A quick assessment of a student's understanding of a particular concept or skill, and a check for understanding. A guide to planning instruction.

Procedure:

After a lecture of a new concept or skill or information, give each student a three-by-five card.

Students write their name and answer questions, typically three or four, posted on board or overhead by the teacher.

Should not take more than five minutes.

Scenario

A sixth grade social studies teacher has just finished lecturing on the ancient Egyptian social class structure. The questions shown in Exhibit 4.1 are on the overhead and the students are handed a three-by-five card.

Tips:

• Before completing their first exit card, complete a model with students to establish your expectations.

Exhibit 4-1
Questions on the Overhead

DIRECTIONS:

Answer each question on the supplied card to the best of your ability.

1. Which class of people were the highest (most important) in the ancient Egyptian social class?

2. Which class of people were the lowest (least important) in the ancient Egyptian social class?

3. On a scale of 1 to 4 (4 means you understand everything), rate your understanding of today's lecture.

When you are finished, please put the cards face down on your desk and I will come around and collect them.

- Explain rating scale (if using one) and give examples of each level the first few times, completing exit cards.
- Always tell the students what to do with cards when finished.

Adaptations:

- Vary the thinking skills levels of the questions according to Bloom's taxonomy.
- Use five-by-seven cards for younger grades or students with fine motor difficulties.
- Type or write out questions prior to lesson, or write questions that are based on students' questions during lecture.
- Use behavior rating questions: "How good was your on-task behavior during this activity? Explain."
- For older students: "What concepts, words, or problems do you need some further help with?"

Roaming Checklists   A roaming checklist is an informal means of assessment that can be done while the teacher "roams" the room checking on student progress.

These checklists can be made for a number of content areas with varying levels of assessment. One common way we use checklists is to print a class roster from our gradebook program (or simply write the students' names on a piece of paper). Keep the class list on a clipboard for easy use and recording purposes.

While students are working on an independent activity, roam around the room with your clipboard, checking off student progress on the given assignment. It may be a quick stop by a student's desk as she solves an algebra equation; it may be kneeling down next to a student's desk during silent reading time to listen to him whisper-read for one minute to ensure that he is reading a book at an appropriate level; or it could be used to grade participation. Whatever you use it for, it is an easy, flexible, personalized assessment tool.

We have included a variety of grammar and spelling checklists on the following pages as examples of a roaming checklist. In these cases, we have one checklist for every student, and it is used as a method for tracking and recording the student's progress in grammar.

Knowing and keeping track of where your students are and where to take them next is an important first step for differentiating curriculum. As Jay McTighe and Grant Wiggins recommend, begin with the assessments. The next steps involve identifying the skills students require if they are to be successful in a given learning task.

Informal Writing Prompts and Review Questions   We use writing prompts and review questions in our classes virtually every day. Whether or not the prompts and questions are graded must be left to the teacher's discretion, and he or she must decide what the purpose of the prompt or question is: final assessment, a guide for further instruction, or both.

We use writing prompts to process recently learned content or to get students thinking about upcoming, new content. Examples of writing prompts:

- How would you explain the difference between myosis and meitosis? (process newly learned information)

Exhibit 4-2
Pronoun Checklist

PURPOSE: Monitoring progress of advanced students who are working at their own pace through grammar exercises

Have a teacher initial the section *before* going on to the next section.

Grammar Assignment	Teacher Initials
Exercise A: Pronouns and antecedents	_____
Exercise A: Personal pronouns	_____
Exercise B: Reflexive and intensive	_____
Exercise C: Demonstrative and interrogative	_____
Exercise A: Indefinite and relative	_____
Exercise B: Indefinite and relative	_____

Adaptations:

- Label clearly what page (if using grammar program) each exercise is on.
- If creating worksheets, have them available in file folders for student access.
- Caution: use only if appropriate on basis of preassessment and knowing students' learning style.

- What was the highlight of your weekend? (prepare for discussion)
- Tell me about the conflict your main character faces. (processing and preparing for discussion)
- What do you know about Rome? (prepare for new unit)

Review questions are teacher- or text-generated questions that assess student understanding of newly learned material, such as "Give an example of a rational number and an irrational one." Again, these may be graded or not.

Teachers need to determine how to best incorporate writing prompts and review questions to further student learning. How they are used might change from day to day, according to student need, subject matter, or lesson design.

Short Quizzes Short quizzes consist of no more than five questions that tell the teacher what the students have learned. We give them throughout a unit to assess student understanding before progressing to a new concept.

Student Surveys Student surveys are either oral or written. Here is an example of a quick survey: "If you feel you could explain adding decimals to a new student in this class, show a thumbs up. If you think you understand it but not enough to teach it, show a thumb sideways. If you don't feel ready at all, and you may need help from me, please show a thumbs down." The teacher then counts "one, two, three" and on three all students show thumbs at the same time. With a quick glance, the teacher notes thumbs-down students, whom she can then reteach while the other students work on independent or guided practice. Other surveys might be in the form of a checklist, regarding student skills, learning preferences, and likes and dislikes. Surveys are used to assess student level of understanding before, during, and after a lesson.

Worksheet 4-1
Sample Checklists for Teacher Records of Student Progress

Student Name:

Spelling Skill	Test Date	Score	Words Incorrect	Test Date	Score	Words Incorrect	% Mastery
Short o Short e Short i Short u Short a Long o Long e (y) Long i (y) Vowel sound: ee Vowel sound: ea Vowel sound: ai Vowel sound: ay Vowel sound: ow Vowel sound: ue Vowel sound: ui Vowel sound: ew Vowel sound: oo Vowel sound: ou Vowel sound: au, ou, aw o-consonant-eu-consonant-e -ir, -er, -ur, -ar Consonant blends: sw-, sp-, scr-, spl- Consonant blend: th-, wh-, sh-, ch- Compound words Contractions							

Worksheet 4-2
Examples of Flexible Grouping

Sample

Name

Dates assessed in appropriate boxes:

Grammar Skill	Reteach	Making Progress	Mastered
Nouns			
Common			
Proper			
Compound subjects			

Bloom's Taxonomy: A Quick Review

We learn about Bloom's taxonomy in our teacher education programs. The philosophy is worth reviewing when considering the easiest way to get started in differentiating curriculum. It is based on the understanding that students feel (and are) most successful if they are initially given a chance to experience success. Help them warm up with questions you know they can answer first. For those kids who are turning off to such fundamental questions, challenge them by beginning a bit higher on the spiral. Asking spiraling questions is similar to learning how to play soccer.

Learning to Play Soccer	Asking Engaging Questions
Roll your ankles around, breathe deeply, and stretch your upper body before beginning your warm-up run.	Begin questioning students with the most fundamental, *knowledge-based* questions, recalling information that can be found on the page. This is safe, and any student can be successful.
Dribble a soccer ball up and down the field, jogging slowly to warm up your reflexes and your heart.	Move on to asking *comprehension* questions that demonstrate a student's understanding of the content material. Again, this is safe, and most students will be successful with this level of questioning, for which they can look back in the text for reference if necessary.

Pass the ball back and forth with a partner.

Now you are ready to pick up the pace and challenge just a bit. At this level, students must *apply* newly learned knowledge to something else they know, whether a procedure, a product, or a line of thinking.

Continue passing the ball back and forth while running up and down the length of the field.

Analytical questioning requires students to begin picking apart the new knowledge to make sense of it. They must not only start thinking outside the box (and off the page of text) but use critical thinking skills and create meaning for themselves.

Practice running the ball past defensive players and take a shot at the goal.

By bringing many learned skills together, students *synthesize* information. They connect newly learned information with other knowledge, and adjust as necessary.

Reflect on the skills and plays you just practiced. Decide what you did well, and which skills or strategies you must still work on to score a goal.

Evaluative questions require students to make judgment calls on new information. They must know themselves well and feel comfortable sharing and defending a position when answering these high-level, critical thinking questions.

The easiest place to start implementing differentiation is with questioning. A list of leveled skills and question starters based on Bloom's taxonomy is in Exhibit 4.3. We recommend you start with whole-class discussions; no doubt you realize that you already do ask spiraled questions without even recognizing this is what you do. It is simply good teaching practice. Eventually, you can tier assignments according to students' critical thinking ability.

Designing Differentiated Questions

Practice designing questions that fit into the categories we created earlier, in Chapter Three: grade level (GL), foundational (*), and advanced grade level (AGL). Depending on course content, topic concepts, and skills being addressed at any given time, students can fall into any of the categories. For instance, Madeleine might be a very high-level thinker in grasping new math concepts such as integers (AGL), but when it comes to social studies concepts in history, such as democracy, she may struggle in the realm of application (GL or possibly *). This is where preassessment is such a valuable tool in helping you design how students will practice skills and learn the necessary content at a proficient (or higher) level.

For any content area reading assignment or class discussion, we can group questions into three categories, described in Exhibit 4.4. Note that Bloom's levels are not so finely delineated; rather, they may fall into more than one category of questioning.

Exhibit 4-3
Bloom's Taxonomy: A Review

Knowledge

Recall	Label	Find	Match
Which	Define	Name	List
Who is ...?	What is ...?	Where is ...?	
Why does ...?	How does ...?	When is ...?	

Comprehension

Relate	Interpret	Rephrase
Classify	Explain	Demonstrate

What facts or ideas show ...?
Which statements support ...?
How would you compare ...? Contrast ...?
What is the main idea of ...?
How would you summarize ...?

Application

Utilize	Experiment with	Construct	Identify
Apply	Plan	Develop	Select

How would you solve ...?
What would result if ...?
What questions would you ask in an interview with ...?
How would you organize ... to show ...?
What approach would you use to ...?
What elements would you choose to change ...?

Analysis

Distinguish	Simplify	Test for	Discover
Disect	Analyze	Assume	

What inference can you make ...?
What motive is there ...?
How would you classify or categorize ...?
What conclusions can you draw ...?
What ideas justify ...?

Synthesis

Elaborate	Compile	Construct	Imagine
Adapt	Estimate	Propose	Choose

What alternative can you propose to …?
What could be done to minimize or maximize …?
What could be combined to improve or change …?
Can you invent or formulate a model or theory for …?
Suppose you could …; what would you do …?
Can you predict the outcome if …?

Evaluation

Criticize	Justify	Defend	Perceive
Interpret	Deduce	Dispute	

What is your opinion of …?
How would you assess the value or importance of …?
What would you recommend for …?
What choice would you have made …?
Explain why you do or don't agree with the actions of …?

Adapted from Nancy Craig Workshop

Differentiated Thinking Activities

You can apply differentiated questioning techniques to skills:

- As an exit card assessment at the end of the day (plan for next day's instruction)
- As a warm-up activity
- As homework or in-class practice

Maureen first began consciously designing differentiated lessons in her "literature letters":

I used to give just one prompt for every student to address each week. Now I provide three or four levels of prompts, challenging students who can handle it and creating a more accessible learning opportunity for students struggling with literary elements and response. I made it clear to students that I expected them to choose the prompt best suited to their individual level, conferencing and guiding them as needed. My written responses to student literature letters would question, challenge, and encourage every student.

Reading Classwork or Homework

Example A: Literature Letter Prompts
Choose one of the prompts below and write a letter. Begin by introducing the book you are reading and who the author is. Your letter should have an introductory

paragraph (title, author, setting, main idea) and one or two body paragraphs that address the prompt.

Character

1. Describe the physical and personality traits of the main character in your story. (*)

2. Who is the main character, and what is the problem (conflict) she is facing? How do you think she will solve the conflict? (predict resolution; GL)

3. Explain how a character or situation in the story reminds you of some person or event in your life. Be as specific as possible. (AGL)

Reading Classwork or Homework

Example B: Literature Letter Prompts

Choose one of the prompts below and write a letter. Begin by introducing the book you are reading and who the author is. Your letter should have an introductory paragraph (title, author, setting, main idea) and one or two body paragraphs that address the prompt.

Setting

1. How would the story be different if it were set in McKinleyville in 2003? (AGL)

2. What elements of the story's setting would you change to improve the main character's condition? (GL)

3. Describe the setting of the story (please include both time and place). (*)

4. How does the story's setting affect plot and character development? (GL)

It took some practice at first, but eventually, with clipboard in hand, I am now able to circulate around the room as students write and I make sure they choose the appropriate level. I then record the letter of the prompt on the clipboard for reference when I read their letters. If necessary, I can guide a student to choose a more challenging prompt. If a student has picked one that I think might be too difficult, I can discuss it with him and carry out the necessary scaffolding to ensure his success. With adequate community building at the beginning of the year, it should not seem at all odd to students that they are selecting different questions to answer. The level identifications are included here for reference only; the students do not see them.

Here are some examples of differentiated math skills practice:

Math Warm-up or Exit Card

Sample A

(*) $1/2 \times 2\ 3/5 =$
(GL) $5 \times -2/3 =$
(AGL) $(2^2 + 6)^2 =$

Bonus: $\dfrac{3 - 2(5 - 1) + 3}{9 - 7} =$

Math Warm-up or Exit Card
    Sample B
    (GL) 3 2/3 × 5/8 =
    (AGL) 1/3 × −7 =
    (*) 1/8 × 2/5 =

Flexible Grouping

Among all the critical components of differentiation, flexible grouping throughout the day and the school year can be one of the most challenging, yet most valuable, parts of a child's learning experiences (Tomlinson, 1999). In the traditional system, from an early age students stigmatize each other and themselves according to the leveled groups they work in during the school day. Flexible grouping allows constant change in the classroom and eliminates the chance of a student associating himself with only one group—high, low, or middle.

Flexibly grouping students not only discourages labeling within the classroom but allows the teacher or teachers to work with individuals or small groups, providing direct instruction that meets their specific needs.

Students who demonstrate mastery of grade level skills can work independently or in small groups on teacher-designated or student's choice enrichment activities (of greater depth and complexity in the subject area). Meanwhile, the teacher can work with students who need extra support. Conversely, students who need extra skill practice may work individually or in small groups while the teacher works with AGL students in small groups on activities of greater depth or complexity. We group students by assessing their learning as often as possible.

Assessment to Guide Flexible Grouping

In the differentiated classroom, use assessments to help you with flexible grouping. As we have tried to make clear, flexible grouping is vital to both student academic success and self-esteem. In our experience, and that of our colleagues, static grouping creates stereotypes among students.

Exhibit 4-4
Differentiated Questioning

FIND IT! (foundational level)
    This is a question that can be answered by any student who can read or find it on the page. It is explicit. (knowledge or comprehension)

COMPARE IT! (grade level)
    This is a question that can be answered by a student who reads between the lines. It is implicit. (comprehension, application, or analysis)

OWN IT! (advanced grade level)
    This is a question that can be answered by any student who is ready and willing to think outside the box. It is sophisticated and requires higher critical thinking. (analysis, synthesis, or evaluation)

Exhibit 4-5
Examples of Flexible Grouping

Type of Grouping	Criteria to Consider	Instructional or Learning Goals
Heterogeneous	• Multiple intelligences, learning styles • Student interests • Random	• Discussion • Final product following whole-class lesson, activity, or unit • Cooperative learning
Readiness (ability) level	• Reading • Spelling • Writing • Conceptual or organizational	• Skills-based small group • Skills-based individual work
Whole group	• Could everyone here benefit?	• Introducing new concept or unit • Community building activities

Before designing an actual differentiated lesson or activity, keep in mind the true basics: the *skills* students need to be successful in the learning task, the *resources* that support them at their skill level, and the *means of assessment* (or final product) that demonstrate what the student has learned and what he needs to learn next.

It is worth sharing that, for us, the idea of gathering multiple levels of reading material was a tremendous "Ah ha!" moment. Many of our students struggle with reading grade-level content area textbooks. Many are unable to read and comprehend certain Web sites or an encyclopedia—not to mention the dictionary! We now work closely with our librarian and seek out a variety of leveled reading materials whenever possible. Collaboration allows us to share the many resources we find buried deep within our cupboards, including brand new sample textbooks. Co-teaching with a special education expert opens the door to all kinds of graphic organizers and modified textbooks that give a struggling reader access to the information he or she needs to learn.

Chapter Five

Sample Lessons, Activities, and Templates

And now, the nitty-gritty. On the next pages, we address the nuts and bolts of differentiation and offer examples of actual lessons and templates.

Tiered Assignments

A tiered assignment is an ability-driven instructional and learning tool. It is the type of assignment we create only in instances where we decide that students will greatly benefit from such an assignment. Following preassessment, the teacher establishes grade-level, foundational, and advanced grade level groups for a particular content standard. The teacher then determines appropriate skills, resources, and end products (a means of assessment) for the group so that each student may maximize his or her individual learning potential. The teacher plans out the leveled activities on the template and writes up corresponding assignments for the students. We always begin at grade level and then either modify for the foundational learner or enrich for those students needing a greater challenge. A reproducible planning template (Worksheet 5.1) follows several samples (Exhibits 5.1 through 5.3).

Creating Tiered Assignments

Step one: determine thematic big idea or essential question (one that students refer to throughout various units during the year).

Step two: identify grade level or content area standard.

Step three: identify topic of study, such as earthquake faults.

Step four: decide how you will assess students' prior knowledge of topic so you do not assume too much. For example, some students may already know quite a bit about earthquake faults and therefore need to be assigned a more in-depth or accelerated curriculum lesson. Others may know less than anticipated and require some very fundamental direct instruction.

Step five: refer to preassessment so as to group students into grade level (expected amount of background knowledge of topic), foundational (minimal, erroneous, or no background knowledge), or advanced grade level (ready for acceleration or in-depth study).

Step six: determine the skills each group must master by the end of the lesson. We state these skills in question form (critical questions) for ease of discussion with students along with their respective learning objectives.

Step seven: list resources each group will access to obtain information.

Step eight: determine an appropriate means of assessment for each group to produce that will show mastery of skills.

Step nine: anticipate next steps for students who are ready to move on and for students who are not.

Exhibit 5-1
Sample Tiered Activity Plan (Teacher's Copy)

Seventh Grade Social Studies

Larger unit, big idea, essential questions: How are historical events influenced by physical geography? (beginning of unit)

GL standard: analyze the geographic structures of Medieval Islam (Ss 7.2)

Topic of study: origins and expansion of Islam

Preassessment and background: exit cards, KWHL class discussion, and text walk

	Grade Level (GL)	**Foundational (*)**	**Advanced Grade level (AGL)**
Critical questions	Can student make use of the facts given to persuade people to visit the region? (*apply*)	Can student *label* the map?	Can student *assess* the significance of a feature?

Resources	• *Across the Centuries* • Blank area map • List of geographical features and associated map key • Islam book cart (supplemental books for unit) • Model travel brochures	• *Across the Centuries* • Blank area map • List of geographical features and associated map key	• *Across the Centuries* • Blank area map • List of geographical features and associated map key • Islam book cart (supplemental books for unit) • Model business letter
Means of assessment (what student will produce to show learning)	Label all geographic features from the list. Create a travel brochure (complete with a labeled map of the region) that will persuade foreigners to come to the Arabian Peninsula to trade. (Consider features, climate, natural resources, and food supply. What do you have available for trade? What would make living in this area desirable?)	Complete a labeled area map, following color code, spelling, and map key requirements. Write a paragraph describing the climate of the area and the resources available for a family to survive (housing, food). Write a second paragraph that persuades a traveler to either stay or move on because of the resources available.	Think of a physical feature that is developing on the Arabian Peninsula that could positively *and* negatively affect the civilizations there. Write a professional business letter to the government convincing them to hire you for designing a new map of the region.
Where next	• What is lacking? • Where or how might you travel for what you need? • Why might a powerful culture evolve here?	• What is lacking? • Where or how might you travel for what you need? • Why might a powerful culture evolve here?	• Where or how might you travel for what you need? • Why might a powerful culture evolve here? • Current event (evolution)

(*Continued*)

Exhibit 5-1 (Continued)

Estimated length of activity (minutes, periods, days): 2 50-min. periods

You will notice in the critical questions boxes that we have italicized thinking-level skills, going back to Bloom's taxonomy. These questions are for us, the educators, to keep in mind what skill level the student should be using to learn the new information (a grade-level standard). Also, this is clearly an assignment that takes into consideration language skills as well: persuasive writing and writing formats. The assignment was based on earlier assessments of writing and student learning preferences (writing, drawing, and so forth). The lesson addresses the interests and talents of one particular class. It is not the kind of lesson we would design and use every week! It was given at the beginning of the unit to engage students and get them thinking about the material they will be studying for the next few weeks. Your tiered assignments can be as simple or as complex as you like.

The resulting three student assignments given here look similar and basically require the same amount of work. The last thing we want to do is turn off a student who is capable of doing more challenging assignments by giving more work.

The assignments students receive are not actually labeled foundational, grade-level, or advanced grade level. What matters is that the teacher keeps track of who gets which assignment. Again, the impact of community building and the idea of everyone having individual strengths and needs should eliminate negative comparison of assignments.

Sample Student Assignment: GL

Name: _____

How Are Historical Events Influenced by Physical Geography?
Analyzing the Geographic Structures of Medieval Islam (SS 7.2)

Topic of study: origins and expansion of Islam
Materials:

- Across the Centuries, pp. _____
- Blank area map of the Middle East
- List of geographical features and associated map key
- Islam book cart
- Model travel brochures

Your Assignment:

1. Label all geographic features from the list on the map.

2. Create a travel brochure (complete with your labeled map of the region) that will persuade foreigners to come to the Arabian Peninsula to trade. (Consider features, climate, natural resources, and food supply. What do you have available for trade? What would make living in this area desirable?)

Sample Student Assignment: *

Name: _____

How Are Historical Events Influenced by Physical Geography?
Analyzing the Geographic Structures of Medieval Islam (SS 7.2)

Topic of study: origins and expansion of Islam
Materials:

- Across the Centuries, pp. _____
- Blank area map of the Middle East
- List of geographical features and associated map key

Your Assignment:

1. Complete a labeled area map, following color code, spelling, and map key requirements.

2. Write a paragraph (minimum five sentences) describing the climate of the area and the resources available for a family to survive (housing, food, and so on).

3. Write a second paragraph that persuades a traveler to either stay or move on because of the resources available.

Sample Student Assignment: AGL

Name: _____

How Are Historical Events Influenced by Physical Geography?
Analyzing the Geographic Structures of Medieval Islam (SS 7.2)

Topic of study: origins and expansion of Islam
Materials:

- Across the Centuries, pp. _____
- Blank area map of the Middle East
- List of geographical features and associated map key
- Islam book cart
- Model business letter

Your Assignment:

1. Think of a physical feature that is developing on the Arabian Peninsula, one that could positively *and* negatively affect the civilizations there.

2. Write a professional business letter to the government convincing them to hire you for designing a new map of the region.

You must explain how this new feature will have an impact on the daily lives of both nomadic and settled people.

With your letter, include a map that shows the new feature and all of the geographic features from your original list.

Exhibit 5-2
Sample Tiered Activity Plan (Teacher's Copy)

Earth Sciences (Level: High School)

Larger unit, big idea: Earth's place in the universe

9–12 Earth Sciences State Standard 1 (essential question form): How has the solar system evolved and changed over time?

Topic: similarities and differences among sun and planets

Preassessment: three-way Venn diagram

Create a three-way Venn diagram for the main types of bodies in the solar system: the sun, the nine terrestrial planets, and the thousands of other bodies. List as many attributes as possible for each. List similar attributes in the intersections.

After establishing the basic background knowledge of her students regarding the solar system, the teacher will provide some whole-class vocabulary, instruction, and reading before assigning the tiered activities shown. The students completing the foundational activity would have shown in the preassessment a limited amount of background knowledge with regard to the solar system and would need scaffolding of basic facts. The grade-level activity students would have shown in that same pre-assessment that they have limited or incorrect background information that must be supplemented or corrected, and they could do this at a higher level of critical think-ing by comparing and contrasting the types of bodies. Students who complete the advanced grade level activity might also still need some supplemental or corrected information, but they have shown the teacher in the past that they grasp facts quickly and can more easily apply knowledge at a higher, evaluative level. Once they have completed this particular activity, both the GL and AGL students will be back on the same learning level. This is an example of flexible grouping at work.

Tiered Activities

	Grade Level	**Foundational**	**Advanced Grade Level**
Critical questions	How would you explain the evolution of similarities and differences among the structure and scales of the sun, the terrestrial planets, and the other bodies?	How can you explain the origin of the solar system? What are the characteristics of the solar system?	Which terrestrial planet would you most like to visit, and which would you least like to visit? Be sure to include specific examples of structure and scale in your explanation.

Resources	Class text Encyclopedia	Class text Eyewitness texts	Class text Encyclopedia Posted news articles
Means of assessment (product)	Choice: • Cartoon • Essay • Poster	Choice: • Cartoon • Essay • Poster	Choice: • Cartoon • Essay • Poster
Where next	Describe the differences in the creation of and life cycles among stars.	Explain the evolution of similarities and differences among the structure and scale of the sun, the terrestrial planets, and the other bodies.	Describe the differences in the creation of and life cycles among stars.

Estimated length of activity (minutes, periods, days): 2 50-min. class periods; 2 nights' homework

Exhibit 5-3
Sample Tiered Activity Plan (Teacher's Copy)

U.S. History (Level: High School)

Larger unit, big idea, essential questions: evolution of U.S. Government

GL standard: 12.5 (students summarize landmark U.S. Supreme Court interpretations)

Topic of study: U.S. Supreme Court

Preassessment: exit card detailing knowledge about Supreme Court and landmark cases

	Grade Level	**Foundational**	**Advance Grade Level**
Critical questions	How has the U.S. Supreme Court's interpretation of the Constitution changed in regard to judicial activism and judicial restraint? Cite specific cases listed on handout.	How have the basic freedoms (religion, speech, press, petition, and assembly) changed over time?	How would you evaluate the arguments espoused by each side? (See handout.) How do these examples of changes in interpretation of the Constitution prove that it is a living document?

(Continued)

Exhibit 5-3 (Continued)

Resources	• Textbook • Handout of landmark Supreme Court cases	• Textbook • Handout of Supreme Court cases • Fifth and eighth grade U.S. history text	• Textbook • Handout of Supreme Court cases • Contemporary Supreme Court cases
Means of assessment	• Essay • Role-play a CNN interview • Comic strip	• Captioned poster • Essay • Role play	• Essay • Role-play CNN inter-view re: current case • Comic strip
Where next	How would you evaluate the arguments espoused by each side? (See handout.) How do these examples of changes in interpretation of the Constitution prove that it is a living document?	Define *judicial activism* and *judicial restraint.* How has the U.S. Supreme Court's interpretation of the Constitution changed in regard to judicial activism and judicial restraint?	Debate

Estimated length of activity (minutes, periods, days): 3 50-min. periods; homework

It is worth noting here that, early on in the school year, we invite students to talk to us at any time about their comfort level on any assignment. At times we have had students complain that an assignment is too hard. If we believe the student is indeed capable of completing the assignment, instead of reassigning the easier one we explain that it is to her advantage to push herself, and that we would be doing her a disservice if we allowed her to do anything less than that. We assure such students that we will furnish the necessary support along the way.

Conversely, we have had students who want to do a higher-level assignment that interests them. Even though the skills required to complete the assignment as it is written may be far too difficult for such a student to be successful, we modify it accordingly and offer as much scaffolding as possible to allow the child the opportunity to try the more challenging assignment.

As always, flexibility matters in the differentiated classroom. Another crucial point to keep in mind when differentiating: "more work" does not mean "more challenge." Students definitely take note of assignments that differ in length and the amount of time required. Marcy Howe, a sixth grade GE teacher on our staff, shares her experience:

Worksheet 5-1
Tiered Activity Teacher Planning Template

Larger unit, big idea, essential questions: _____

GL standard: _____

Topic of study: _____

Preassessment: _____

	Grade Level	Foundational	Advance Grade Level
Critical questions			
Resources			
Means of assessment			
Where next			

Estimated length of activity (minutes, periods, days): _____

Differentiation has given me the skills to challenge all students in a heterogeneous classroom. It's made me aware of the options I have in working with students of differing abilities. I took the opportunity in two consecutive summers to take part in the differentiation training offered by Nancy Craig. Fortunately, our district was very supportive in providing this class. It really has changed my style of teaching. I guess I didn't have a name for differentiating. I did do it to some degree, but I admit that it was not the most thought-out part of my curriculum. Now it's second nature. Each year I get better at modifying several of my projects or lessons.

I remember several years ago I was aware of having two very "gifted" students in my classroom. I decided that I'd "challenge" them by giving them a creative assignment. It turned out that what I was really doing was giving them more work. I heard one of them exclaim, "Do we really have to do this?" If fact, one student never did it.

Again, another example is when I tried to level my spelling. I unintentionally created more work for the higher kids. I had students knowingly misspell words on their pretests just so they wouldn't get the "advanced" packet. A mother told me what was going on. I guess I learn the hard way, but these scenarios stick with me when I differentiate now.

After learning about what *challenge* really means, I know how to level assignments so that it's not more work but just different.

Adapting Curriculum To Meet Student Needs

Exhibit 5.4 suggests just a few ways to adapt your curriculum to meet the variety of student needs in a class. This is in no way an exhaustive list. We have simply gotten you started with some ideas. Mix and match activities according to learning objectives, student need, and student choice.

Exhibit 5-4
Ways to Adapt Your Curriculum to Meet Student Needs

Resources	Skills	Means of assessment
Text	List	Drama
Internet	Identify	Poster
Magazine or news articles	Classify	Written paper
CD-ROM	Compare and contrast	Illustrations
Adopted program software	Deduce	Comic strips
(History Alive! Holt	Prioritize	Demonstration
Language Arts CDs;	Predict	Microsoft PowerPoint
encyclopedias; or Tom		
Snyder geography		
programs, inspiration, etc.)		
Community field trips		
Guest speakers		

Note Taking

As Kevin Feldman and Kate Kinsella (2005) suggest in their research article "Narrowing the Language Gap," leaving blank key words in note taking lessons helps those students who struggle with vocabulary: "In this way students can focus their attention on comprehending the explanation and examples, instead of getting bogged down in the writing process and missing vital context."

In Exhibit 5.5, we share a modified social studies note taking lesson in which we supply most of the notes but omit the key concepts or vocabulary terms. As the teacher lectures, every student takes notes on a notes page, either modified or not, according to need. The student with the modified notes still has to follow along but is focused on the content and on the key concepts and vocabulary terms rather than feeling pressured to "get everything down."

Exhibit 5-5
Social Studies Modified Notes

surrounded on _____ sides by water;

good for _____ and _____ Strait made the city

control of _____;

a shipping and _____ hub

capital of _____ Roman Empire;

heavily influenced by _____ culture;

just like Rome, built on _____ hills and

divided into _____ districts

protected by _____ miles of wall,

watchtowers, and _____;

walls only needed to be built on

_____ side of the city

survived centries of _____,

religious discord, _____, and

_____ leaders;

seized by _____ in 1453 and

renamed _____; today it is

a major city in Modern _____

As previously mentioned, it is crucial that everyone understand why certain students get modified notes and others do not. This all goes back to creating a sense of community in your classroom. After seven years and creating a schoolwide culture where everyone gets what they need, we rarely hear students complain. It is just how it is.

It is important to note in conclusion that we do not create tiered assignments for every lesson. We use them when, following preassessment, we find that our students have wide-ranging knowledge about a particular topic. For students to be successful in mastering the identified standard, we use the tiered assignment to allow them access to either below-grade-level or advanced reading material. In addition, students learn the standard by using a skill that is appropriate to their needs. Finally, the product, or means of assessment, varies with student interest, or in some cases it may not vary at all (for example, an end-of-unit test). The next chapters offer additional examples of how to adapt curriculum to meet student needs that are not quite as work-intensive as the tiered assignment. Reading bookmarks, addressed in Chapter Six, are one such instance. This is a flexible way to address a variety of reading levels in one classroom that can be used throughout the school year.

Chapter Six

Contracts and Menus

We love contracts and menus for a number of reasons. Simply using the name *contract* implies a need for responsibility and student commitment. And who doesn't like the implication of a menu? The two can be used in isolation or in combination (as seen in Exhibit 6.3), but in either case the format you create can be used again and again throughout the year, with minor modification as topics of study change.

A contract is an instructional and learning tool that offers students choice within teacher-designated parameters. Students acknowledge their responsibility to complete the assignment within a given amount of time.

A menu is an instructional and learning tool that offers students choice within teacher-designated parameters. Students complete a combination of teacher-assigned "must do's" and student-choice "choose to do's." It is called a menu because, as in a restaurant, students get to choose their order.

Spelling and Word Study Contracts

Time and time again within our own school and at numerous workshops, the issue of how to differentiate spelling has comes up. Some teachers have reduced the amount of words for struggling spellers, some have increased words for the gifted students, and others simply teach to the middle.

Whether you have a state-adopted spelling program or generate your own lists, we have created multileveled spelling contracts which are successful with various student ability levels in one classroom. We have also found that by middle school the mere word *spelling* creates a sense of dread among those students for whom spelling is not a strength. In addition, we believe that students should not only spell words correctly but also understand the meaning of the words and be able to use them correctly in the context of sentences. So with a simple change of semantics, our "spelling" is now "word study," which also incorporates vocabulary development and use of words in context.

Creating Word Study Contracts

Step 1: Preassess

As with any unit of study, the first step is to determine what your students already know. We give oral spelling pretests of words the day before we want to start a unit so we can level the students. In the Word Study Unit Two contract, we focused on five common Greek and Latin root words. For differing ability levels, you can furnish the words as shown on the contract (see Exhibit 6.3 later in this chapter), or you can have the students generate words with the given roots.

Step 2: Connect to Spelling Skill for the Week

When we originally created Word Study Unit Two: Greek and Latin Roots (Exhibit 6.2), we noticed in our students' papers that they were having a difficult time understanding the rules of forming plural nouns. This was the spelling skill for the week. A minilesson confirmed the students' need for further instruction in forming plural nouns. After introducing the Greek and Latin root words, using guided instruction in a whole-class setting, we applied the spelling skill for the week. Students first had to identify which words were nouns and write the plurals of those words in the boxes, following the rules for forming plural nouns.

This kind of lesson and practice can be done in a variety of grouping formats. Students can independently practice as a whole class or in pairs. The preassessment may show that the foundational students require a teacher-provided list of rules for reference as they complete the assignment.

Please note that not all the boxes will be used and this also may be adapted for the foundational level students by only providing as many boxes as needed for forming plural nouns. In any practice format, the teacher can use the finished product as a follow-up assessment.

Step 3: Personal Words

This section has proven to be one of the most successful for all students regardless of their spelling ability. Many teachers have often complained to us, as we have complained to each other throughout the years, about needing to teach grade-level spelling to students who cannot yet spell simple, high-frequency words such as *which* or *because*, or to those students who have aced every spelling test when given words to spell in isolation but once the test is over they continue to misspell the words in their language arts papers. Personal words are taken directly from the context of the student's writing. Each student at the beginning of the year is given a personal word log, which is kept in her binder or writer's workshop folder according to class set-up. After every word study test, students must correct the ones identified as incorrect by the teacher, and write the correctly spelled word in their personal word logs. In addition, any words that the teacher identifies on any written papers, whether they are in a persuasive essay, literature letter, or other writing, must be spelled correctly and written in the personal word log. Here are adaptations for the various levels:

○ **Foundational level** (*): teachers identify five misspelled words at a time so as not to discourage the student. Identify high-frequency words first that the student will likely use again in his writing. On the basis of the student's needs, the teacher could give the correctly spelled word for him rather than have him access a dictionary or other source for the correct spelling.

○ **Grade level (GL):** teachers identify up to ten misspelled words or identify what line the misspelled word is on in the student work by placing an "X" in the margin of the line. The strategy you use depends on the student's need. The student would then read over the words in that line and try to identify the misspelled word.

X In Ancient Rome gladeators were a form of entertainment.

○ Whenever possible, we analyze the student's error and try to find a pattern in the misspelled words, such as errors in vowel combination, prefix or suffix spelling, and so on.

○ **Advanced grade level (AGL):** if there are no misspelled words in the student's writing, the teacher has a variety of resources to promote deeper and more complex word attack skills and vocabulary. For students not using complex words in their writing, identify words they can then look up in a thesaurus to enrich their vocabulary and spelling. For students who are truly advanced in spelling and vocabulary, both in isolation and in the context of their writing, during workshop (small-center time) those students are given a pretest using either our county spelling bee level three words or high-use academic words (K. Feldman). The students self-correct the pretests immediately in workshop with the teacher's assistance. They also need to tell the teacher the word's meaning and use it in a sentence, orally or written, and if unsure they need to look it up in a dictionary.

There are two main reasons we feel that personal spelling lists are of the utmost importance. First, we noticed that students tended to prepare for spelling tests and demonstrate mastery in one shot (writing words in isolation) but then spell the same words incorrectly in their writing, not long after the test was over. Additionally, despite being in middle school, students continued to struggle with high-frequency words, such as *does*, *which*, *because*, and *from*. Such words are now part of our schoolwide No Excuse Spelling Words, posted in every classroom. In most cases, students self-select their personal spelling words from their writing NoDrafts or finals, literature letters, writing prompts, and homework assignments. Students who find few or no errors in their work (as confirmed by a teacher) are challenged to develop their vocabulary through additional study of Greek and Latin roots, the Feldman High Use Academic Words list, a thesaurus, and adopted curriculum extra-challenge spelling words. We help students who struggle to identify misspelled words by placing an X on the line of writing with a misspelled word.

Step 4: Workshop Time with Anchor Activities

The remainder of the contract depends on which lessons are being taught or reviewed that week. We always have a workshop time at least once a week where some students are grouped and meet with a teacher at a side table while the others remain in their seats working on an anchor activity. Grouping students is very important, depending on your instructional objectives for the particular lesson. For anchor activities, we write on a dry erase board or chalkboard the *must do* anchor activities and the *choose to do* activities. This gives the teacher quiet time to work with groups without students asking what to do when they are finished.

Exhibit 6-1
Anchor Activities

Must Do:

- Continue NoDraft number one of personal narrative
- Read silently for 20 minutes, record on your reading log
- Make Science/Social Studies flash cards (if mult. subject)

Choose to Do:

- Free-write a story of your choice (fiction or nonfiction)
- Illustrate your favorite scene from your independent reading book
- Write a review of a movie you saw recently

Step 5: Choice Activities

Students love having choice. The choice activities that we outline allow students to show us they understand the meaning of words rather than just how to spell them correctly. We change

Exhibit 6-2
Word Study Unit Two: Greek and Latin Root Words

Forming the Plurals of Nouns
Due Date: 3/28/06

Hydros: hydroplane, dehydrate, hydrogen, hydrology
aqua: aquarium, aqueduct, aquifer, aquamarine
sol: solar, solarium, solstice, parasol
helios: heliotrope, helium, helioscope
luna: lunar, lunatic, lunacy

Spelling Rules: Forming the Plurals of Nouns
Apply to Vocabulary and Personal Words:

- Personal Words: choose 2 words from your personal word log and write them here: _____
- Thursday: workshop with anchor activities.
- Friday: choice activity (see below). Write spelling words five times each.
- Monday: complete the vocabulary application worksheet. Write each spelling word five times.

Tuesday: Word Study Test Choice Activity Menu

A. Write a minimum three-word alliteration for each spelling word. Alliteration must make sense, and give clues to the word's meaning.	B. Use the Greek and Latin root words to make up words and define them.	C. Create a crossword puzzle; include an answer key.
D. Divide each word into syllables, identify the part of speech, and create derivations for each word.	E. Write a story using all of your words.	F. Create a test for all your words (matching word to definition, multiple choice, etc.); include an answer key.

some of the choice activities every couple of weeks and often include a box offering student choice with teacher approval. In the past, students have chosen to create comic strips, produce an advertisement, or write a poem. As long as they get teacher approval before starting the choice, anything goes (see choice activity menu options in Exhibit 6.5 later in this chapter).

Step 6: Vocabulary Application

Vocabulary application activity can be anything the student does to demonstrate understanding of the meaning of words. For example, it can be as simple as creating a fill-in-the-blank test, writing each word in a sentence, devising a Jeopardy-type game with a partner, making flash cards with student-generated sentences using the words, or having the students complete a worksheet from your state-adopted textbook.

In the contract samples we give here, notice that they look similar despite being for differing levels.

Contract and Menu Style

Depending on teacher and student preferences, contracts may be in linear or boxed-menu format. Although a contract of either style may be differentiated to meet individual student needs, they all should look similar throughout your classroom to avoid any stigmatizing. Your contract must also include precise directions and due dates so that students can be as independent as possible. Students should be familiar with activities and concepts in any contract so that they do not depend on you for instruction. The number of choices you offer is always your decision.

Menu Activities

We have collected the activities seen in Exhibit 6.5 over the years and keep the list handy for creating new menu contracts. You will find that students have their favorites. You will also find that not every option works with every kind of word study. However, there are times when you can use the same options for a number of weeks before rotating in new activities. Before giving such options to students, we recommend that you be sure they have had experience with the activities beforehand. If students choose to write analogies, for instance, but they have never written one before, they will not be able to work independently.

Menu Contract Samples

Throughout the remainder of this section, we share a variety of menu contract samples for teachers, along with their associated student copies. We also include a reproducible teacher planning template.

Word Study Contract A

Due date:
WORD BANK:

- Choose five *personal* spelling words from your word logs.
- Create eight *vocabulary* words from these Greek and Latin roots: *tres* (three) and *quattuo* (four). Examples: tricycle, quadrilateral.
- Two vocabulary words from Chapter 4 (HLLA): foreshadow, resolution

Please write your fifteen words here. Be sure to spell correctly.

1. _____

2. _____

3. _____

4. _____

5. _____

6. _____

7. _____

8. _____

9. _____

10. _____

(Continued)

11. _____

12. _____

13. _____

14. _____

15. _____

MUST DO:

- **Monday:** write each word that **you chose from your personal spelling list** five times on the words practice page.
- **Tuesday:** write a complex or compound "show-not-tell" sentence for your ten vocabulary words (see *Holt Handbook*, pp. 131–137 for examples of complex and compound sentences).

CHOOSE TO DO:

- Always <u>underline</u> and use all your words for the daily practice activities.
- **Thursday:** complete one of the menu activities. Your choice: _____
- **Monday:** complete another of the menu activities. Your choice: _____

Menu Activities

A. Write a story, poem, or song.	**B.** Create a crossword puzzle, including an answer key (counts as two assignments).	**C.** Write a dialogue between at least two people.
D. Write a series of tongue twisters (*alliteration*) showing meaning.	**E.** Design a comic strip or storyboard.	**F.** Write an antonym or synonym for each word.
G. Write a context sentence for each word.	**H.** Write newspaper headlines.	**I.** Create a test and key (matching, multiple choice, etc.).

I understand and will complete this contract to the best of my ability:
_____ (student signature and date)

Name: _____

Word Study Contract B

Due date:

WORD BANK:

- Eight spelling words from Lesson Two: homophones (real, reel, tied, tide, pain, pane, shown, shone)
- Five personal spelling words from your personal word logs (no repeats of above words)
- Two vocabulary words from Chapter 4 (HLLA): foreshadow, resolution

Please write your fifteen words here. Be sure to spell correctly.

1. _____

2. _____

3. _____

4. _____

5. _____

6. _____

7. _____

8. _____

9. _____

10. _____

11. _____

12. _____

13. _____

(*Continued*)

14. _____

15. _____

MUST DO:

- **Monday:** write each word that **you chose from your personal spelling list** five times on the words practice page.
- **Tuesday:** complete the two-sided Spelling Lesson Two: homophones worksheet provided.

CHOOSE TO DO:

- Always <u>underline</u> and use all your words for the daily practice activities.
- **Thursday:** complete one of the menu activities. Your choice:
- **Monday:** complete another of the menu activities. Your choice:

Menu Activities

A. Write a story, poem, or song.	**B.** Create a crossword puzzle, including an answer key (counts as two assignments).	**C.** Write a dialogue between at least two people.
D. Write a series of tongue twisters (*alliteration*) showing meaning.	**E.** Design a comic strip or storyboard.	**F.** Write an antonym or synonym for each word.
G. Write a context sentence for each word.	**H.** Write newspaper headlines.	**I.** Create a test and key (matching, multiple choice, etc.).

I understand and will complete this contract to the best of my ability:
_____ (student signature and date)

Name: _____

Word Study Contract C

Due date:
WORD BANK:

- Ten *spelling* words from Lesson Two: homophones (real, reel, tied, tide, pain, pane, shown, shone, missed, mist)
- Five personal *spelling* words from your personal word logs (no repeats of above words).

Please write your fifteen words here. Be sure to spell correctly.

1. _____

2. _____

3. _____

4. _____

5. _____

6. _____

7. _____

8. _____

9. _____

10. _____

11. _____

12. _____

13. _____

14. _____

15. _____

(Continued)

MUST DO:

- **Monday:** write each word that **you chose from your personal spelling list** five times on the words practice page.
- **Tuesday:** complete the two-sided Spelling Lesson two: homophones worksheet provided.

CHOOSE TO DO:

- Always <u>underline</u> and use all of your words for the daily practice activities.
- **Thursday:** complete one of the menu activities. Your choice:
- **Monday:** complete another of the menu activities. Your choice:

Menu Activities

A. Write a story, poem, or song.	**B.** Create a crossword puzzle, including an answer key (counts as two assignments).	**C.** Write a dialogue between at least two people.
D. Write a series of tongue twisters (*alliteration*) showing meaning.	**E.** Design a comic strip or storyboard.	**F.** Write an antonym or synonym for each word.
G. Write a context sentence for each word.	**H.** Write newspaper headlines.	**I.** Create a test and key (matching, multiple choice, etc.).

I understand and will complete this contract to the best of my ability:

_____ (student signature and date)

Name: _____

Menu A is an example of an AGL contract menu. These students performed exceptionally well on the homophone preassessment. We therefore challenge the student to apply knowledge of Greek and Latin root words, as well as vocabulary words from the current grade-level anthology.

Menu B is a GL contract because of the emphasis on grade-level spelling concept (homophones) as well as vocabulary words from the current grade-level anthology.

Menu C is a foundational contract. Students focus primarily on the grade-level spelling concept (homophones).

Notice that all students are expected to master the grade-level spelling standard concept of homophones (AGL students have already demonstrated mastery through preassessment). All students are required to practice their self-selected spelling words (personal words) as well. Finally, it is important to note that the assignments are similar in appearance and length. AGL students are not expected to do more work than foundational or GL students.

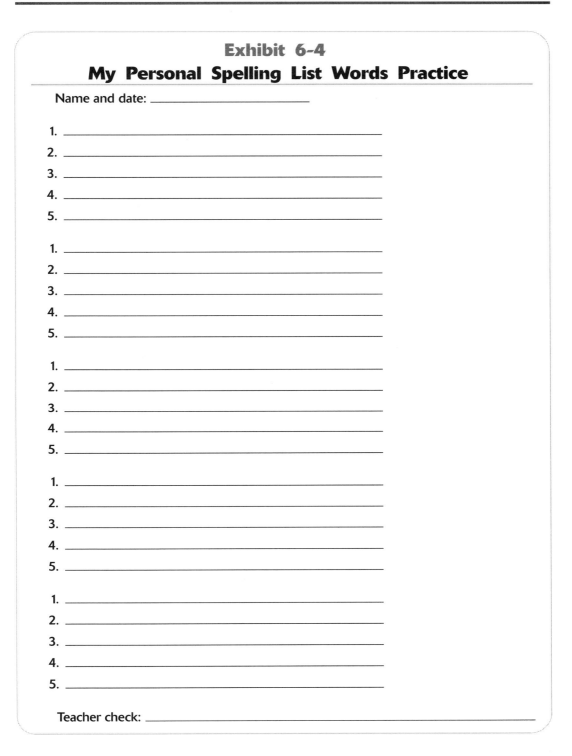

Exhibit 6-4
My Personal Spelling List Words Practice

Name and date: _____

1. _____
2. _____
3. _____
4. _____
5. _____

1. _____
2. _____
3. _____
4. _____
5. _____

1. _____
2. _____
3. _____
4. _____
5. _____

1. _____
2. _____
3. _____
4. _____
5. _____

1. _____
2. _____
3. _____
4. _____
5. _____

Teacher check: _____

Exhibit 6-5
Menu Activities

Alphabetize all of your assigned spelling words.	Divide each of your assigned spelling words into syllables. Use your spelling dictionary.	Write each of your assigned spelling words in cursive *two* times.
Create a picture with all of your assigned spelling words hidden in the images.	Write a story, poem, or song using all of your assigned spelling words. Use proper capitalization and underline your words.	Using all of your spelling words, create a word search. Circle the spelling words.
Write a dialogue between at least two people using ten or more of your words. Be sure there is a beginning, middle, and end to the conversation.	Write a series of tongue twisters (*alliteration*) using all of your spelling words. Underline your words.	Choose ten or more words and create an analogy for each. Underline your words. Analogies can show synonym, antonym, or tool-and-use relationships.
Write a newspaper headline using all of your assigned spelling words. Use proper capitalization.	Create a crossword puzzle using eight to ten of your assigned spelling words. Include key.	Create a proofreading activity with misspelled spelling words. Include a key that shows underlined and properly spelled words.
Create a word scramble, complete with key.	Write a song or poem using all of your assigned spelling words.	Use magazine cutouts or draw pictures to illustrate correctly spelled words.
Classify your spelling words according to parts of speech.	Make word letter cards and find a partner to play spelling word scrabble.	Design a comic strip or storyboard using all your spelling words.
Create similes for all of your spelling words.	Write a context sentence for each word.	Write an antonym or synonym for each spelling word.

Worksheet 6-1
Menu Style Contract Teacher Planning Template

Larger unit, big idea, essential questions: _____

GL standard: _____

Topic of study: _____

Preassessment: _____

Assignment Organizational Chart

	Grade Level (GL)	Foundational (*)	Advanced Grade Level (AGL)
Critical questions			
Students			
Menu activity choices			

Estimated length of activity (minutes, periods, days): _____

Exhibit 6-6
Sample Menu Contract Plan (Teacher Copy)

Sample 1:   Name _____

Independent Reading Contract

During the next three weeks, we will be doing an independent reading contract. Please check the box next to the items you plan on completing.

Must do:

- Read one AR [accelerated reader] book in your ZPD [zone of proximal development], do a book completion form, and pass the computerized test.
- Complete the weekly reading logs for independent reading.

Choose two of the following:

- Do a book project on a novel of your choice.
- Complete six SRA [McGraw Hill strategic reading program] stories.
- Read and complete three workbook stories.
- Present two book recommendations to the class.

Please meet with a teacher to get your contract approved.

Student signature: _____

Teacher signature: _____

Staple this contract on the top of your completed assignments.

Sample 2:

Name/core: _____

Unit: _____

Lesson spelling strategies: _____

_____

_____

Must do: _____

Choose to do from menu: _____

(Over for menu)

Menu

Alphabetize spelling words	Divide each word into syllables	Write a definition for each word	Write one context sentence for each word
Make word letter cards and partner scrabble	Write a synonym for each word	Write an antonym for each word	Create a picture with hidden words
Classify words according to part of speech	Write tongue twisters (*alliteration*) for each word	Create a proofread with all the words	Create a word search
Use the words in similes	Write each word in cursive	Write a story using all the words	Write newspaper headlines using the words
Use magazine cutouts to create a collage of all the words	Write a song or poem using the words	Create a word scramble, complete with key	Make a crossword, complete with key

Exhibit 6-7
Sample Menu Contract Plan
(Teacher and Student Copies)

On the teacher copy that follows, on the basis of the outcome, three background knowledge levels will emerge. Use your Assignment Organizational Chart to keep track of each student's level.

On the student copy that follows, the teacher writes in the menu options available to the students, according to their skill levels or interests.

Seventh Grade Social Studies
Teacher Copy

Larger unit, big idea, essential questions: how does the religion of a civilization contribute to its successes and failures? (beginning of unit)

GL standard: analyze the geographic structures of Medieval Islam (7.2).

Topic of study: origins of Islam and connections with Christianity and Judaism

Preassessment: exit card (day before)

It is always OK if you don't know the answer. Please be a responsible learner and let us know what you do and do not know.

- What are the three monotheistic religions?
- What are two things you know about Islam?

Assignment Organizational Chart
(teacher keeps copy for reference)

	Grade Level (GL)	Foundational (*)	Advanced Grade Level (AGL)
Critical questions	How would you compare and contrast two monotheistic religions?	Why did Muhammad begin the religion of Islam?	If you had been in Muhammad's position, what would you have done with the information you received? Justify your position.
Students	Christy, Samantha, etc.	Jack, etc.	Anna, Brian, etc.
Menu activity choices	C, D (E, F to allow more options if necessary)	A, B	E, F (C, D to allow more options if necessary)

Estimated length of activity: 2 days (1–50-min. period each)

Seventh Grade Social Studies
Student Copy

Student name: _____ Due date: _____

Larger unit, big idea, essential questions: How does the religion of a civilization contribute to its successes and failures?

GL standard: analyze the geographic structures of Medieval Islam (7.2).

Topic of study: origins of Islam and connections with Christianity and Judaism

Must do:

- (WHOLE CLASS) Read *Across the Centuries*, "The Roots of Islam."
- Complete timeline.
- Complete "Monotheistic Religions and Their Fundamental Attributes" chart.
- Word wall vocabulary flashcards.

Choose to do:

Circle one of the options from the menu:

A. Retell the story of Muhammad and the Angel Gabriel in at least two five-sentence paragraphs. You must include at least five vocabulary terms from the word wall.	B. Create a panel comic strip of seven to ten panels with dialogue detailing the story of Muhammad and the Angel Gabriel. You must include at least five vocabulary terms from the word wall.	C. Write a journal entry, with three paragraphs of five sentences or more, from Muhammad's point of view, in which you grapple with that day's events. You are in conflict over the message you received. What will you do with the information? You must include at least seven vocabulary terms from the word wall.
D. Create a diagram or flow chart that outlines the conflict Muhammad experienced on receiving the message from the Angel Gabriel. It should show possible outcomes of the decisions he could have made. You must include at least seven vocabulary terms from the word wall.	E. Choose two of the three monotheistic religions and complete a Venn diagram demonstrating your understanding of the similarities and differences between the two. You must include at least seven vocabulary terms from the word wall.	F. From what you know about the three monotheistic religions, prepare a news conference in which you and two friends answer questions from the class that address the similarities and differences between them. The class will then guess which religion each of you represented.

This lesson has been adapted from an integrated science and math unit created by MaryAnn Sheridan and Jody Himango, seventh and eighth grade teachers at McKinleyville Middle School. It is important to adjust any template to meet a teacher's personal needs. Here, MaryAnn and Jody refer to "critical skills" as opposed to critical questions.

In this lesson, it is assumed that the teachers already know their students' abilities quite well, which is why the AGL students are asked to take the lesson beyond a simple X-Y axis with positives and move immediately into investigating and plotting negative integers as well. These students are expected to determine new relationships, in this case scientific relationships, that result in negative correlations. For example, students might investigate the effects of smoking or drinking alcohol on fetal development. The three groups will receive different assignments, which follow the teacher's organizational chart. Teachers are likely to meet with small groups and furnish reading materials or guidance as necessary. The menu options have been designed so that there are no limitations in final product choice. Any assignment can work with any menu option, so MaryAnn and Jody have leveled assignments by ability and designed means of assessment options by learning style or preference.

Exhibit 6-8
Sample Menu Contract Plan
(Teacher and Student Copies)

Math: statistics and probability
Science: human development
Level: middle and high school

GL standard: statistics and probability

Topics of study: scatter plots (primary), human development (secondary)

Objective: represent two numerical variables on a scatter plot; describe data point distribution and variable relationships.

Preassessment: exit card: What does *correlation* mean (as in, "What is the *correlation* between height and weight")? What is a scatter plot?

Sample Menu Contract Plan (Teacher Copy)
ASSIGNMENT ORGANIZATIONAL CHART

Must do:

- *Measure* heights of body and head in centimeters.
- *Label* heights on T-chart.
- *Create* an X-Y axis graph and *plot* heights.

Choose to do:

	Grade Level (GL)	Foundational (*)	Advanced Grade Level (AGL)
CRITICAL SKILLS	• Measure, label, create, plot. • Investigate and demonstrate how the correlation between body and head height changes over time.	• Measure, label, create, plot. • Demonstrate your understanding of the correlation between body and head height.	• Measure, label, create, plot. • Investigate and demonstrate relationships with opposite correlations (positive and negative integers).
STUDENTS	Rachael, Joe, Tim, Max, Morgan, Steven, Chantel, Stephanie, Marissa	Trevor, Joanna, Michael, Taylor	Emily, Dean, Jonathon, Sasha, Megan, Matt, Beth
Menu activity choices No limit			

Estimated length of activity (minutes, periods, days): 250-min. periods; 2 nights homework

Menu Options

A. Compose a rap or song about correlation between measurements as they appear on a scatter plot, and perform it for the class.	B. Design a poster that demonstrates, through diagrams and captions, the correlation between measurements as they appear on a scatter plot.
C. Investigate and present an oral report on correlations you have identified. Your report should include a visual aid in the form of a scatter plot.	D. Write two paragraphs that define and include *multiple* examples of the words "correlation" and "scatter plot."

(Continued)

Exhibit 6-8 (Continued)

Sample Menu Contract Plan
(GL Student Copy)

Name and period:
Date:
Measure and Scatter
GL standard: statistics and probability
Topics of study: human development (science), scatter plots (math)
Objective: represent two numerical variables on a scatter plot; describe data point distribution and variable relationships.
Must do:

- *Measure* heights of body and head in centimeters.
- *Label* heights on T-chart.
- *Create* an X-Y axis graph and *plot* heights.
- *Investigate* these correlations as they change over time. Ask friends or neighbors of varying ages if you can measure their body and head heights, and then plot them on additional scatter plots. Compare your scatter plots and explain your conclusions.

Choose to do:

Menu options

A. Compose a rap or song about correlation between measurements as they appear on a scatter plot, and perform it for the class.	B. Design a poster that demonstrates, through diagrams and captions the correlation between measurements as they appear on a scatter plot.
C. Investigate and present an oral report on correlations you have identified. Your report should include a visual aid in the form of a scatter plot.	D. Write two paragraphs that define and include *multiple* examples of the words "correlation" and "scatter plot."

Sample Menu Contract Plan
(* Student Copy)

Name and period:
Date:

Measure and Scatter
GL standard: statistics and probability
Topics of study: human development (science), scatter plots (math)
Objective: represent two numerical variables on a scatter plot; describe data point distribution and variable relationships.

Must do:

- *Measure* heights of body and head in centimeters.
- *Label* heights on T-chart.
- *Create* an X-Y axis graph and *plot* heights.

Choose to do:

Menu options

A. Compose a rap or song about correlation between measurements as they appear on a scatter plot, and perform it for the class.	B. Design a poster that demonstrates, through diagrams and captions, the correlation between measurements as they appear on a scatter plot.
C. Investigate and present an oral report on correlations you have identified. Your report should include a visual aid in the form of a scatter plot.	D. Write two paragraphs that define and include *multiple* examples of the words "correlation" and "scatter plot."

Sample Menu Contract Plan
(AGL Student Copy)

Name and period:

Date:

Measure and Scatter

GL standard: statistics and probability

Topics of study: human development (science), scatter plots (math)

Objective: represent two numerical variables on a scatter plot; describe data point distribution and variable relationships.

Must do:

- *Investigate* correlations in human development. Which measurements will result in negative correlations? What are the scientific findings, for instance, regarding the influence of the amount a pregnant woman smokes or drinks on the development of her baby?
- *Create* an X-Y axis graph and *plot* the measurements.

Choose to do:

Menu options

A. Compose a rap or song about correlation between measurements as they appear on a scatter plot, and perform it for the class.	B. Design a poster that demonstrates, through diagrams and captions, the correlation between measurements as they appear on a scatter plot.
C. Investigate and present an oral report on correlations you have identified. Your report should include a visual aid in the form of a scatter plot.	D. Write two paragraphs that define and include *multiple* examples of the words "correlation" and "scatter plot."

Exhibit 6-9
Sample Menu Contract Plan (Teacher Copy)

Earthquake Projects
Level: Middle School
Standard or objective: to demonstrate understanding and describe examples of plate tectonics and its influence on Earth's structure.

1. Everyone must do: #1
2. Choose to do:

1. *Compare* and *contrast* the Richter and Mercalli scales by organizing similarities and differences on a Venn diagram. *List* two similarities or differences for each section. *Resources:* Use textbook, *Earth Changes* book, library books in classroom, and your notes.	2. Create a two- or three-dimensional *model* using classroom materials that demonstrates these plate boundaries: A. Transform B. Convergent C. Divergent D. Subduction zone *Label* each boundary model with its name. *Describe* the movement of each plate boundary. *Resources:* Use textbook, *Earth Changes* book, library books in classroom, and your notes.
3. *Design* and *develop* a brochure or newspaper feature article illustrating evidence for continental drift. *Describe* the evidence you are illustrating. Color is encouraged. Neatness is part of your grade. Include the four pieces of key evidence from your notes. *Resources:* Use textbook, *Earth Changes* book, library books in classroom, and your notes.	4. *Construct* a two or three-dimensional map of a hypothetical Pangea II, illustrating a past Pangea and a future Pangea II on the basis of how continents are presently moving. *Write a summary* at least three paragraphs long as to why the continents have come together as you have mapped them. *Resources:* Use textbook, *Earth Changes* book, library books in classroom, your notes, Pangea puzzle, and Pangea finger puzzle.

Michele Kamprath
Sixth grade science
McKinleyville Middle School

The contract sample in Exhibit 6.10 does not include a menu. It is, however, a contract because students sign an agreement with the teacher saying that they are aware of their responsibilities as learners.

Some colleagues have expressed concern about how time-consuming it must be to create different-leveled assignments each week. It was time-consuming at first, but the results were the payoff. In the video *At Work in the Differentiated Classroom,* Rick Wormeli refers to this time as the "up-front" work. Maureen recalls: "After my first year of offering weekly spelling contracts that meet students' unique spelling needs, 100 percent of my students were consistently passing their spelling tests. Another unexpected benefit I discovered was the independence students experienced as they set weekly minigoals for themselves, making a plan for what part of the spelling contract assignment they would complete each night that week."

Reading Bookmarks

The *reading bookmark* is a tool that we use with various students. For those who just do not like to read, it holds them more accountable than does the standard reading log and lets them know they are responsible for checking in with a teacher to report on progress. The bookmarks can also be used with students who have difficulty with comprehension, giving them a quick way to reflect on what they are reading. Teachers can use this tool to monitor the students' progress. For students with fluency issues, which are often linked to comprehension difficulties, the bookmark keeps them on a determined reading pace at their independent reading levels.

Step one: student or teacher selects a book on the basis of the student's zone of proximal development, independent reading level.

Step two: student reads aloud as teacher takes a one-minute fluency read.

Step three: from the fluency read and prior knowledge about student's comprehension, teacher assigns a number of pages apart at which to place "bookmarks." For example, for a tenth grade student reading at eighty words per minute with poor comprehension, place a bookmark every four pages. You can also gauge how long it should take the student to read four pages of the book, and accordingly assign your due dates.

Step four: student places six colored Post-it notes at each predetermined number of pages. For example, if you want Jack to complete a bookmark every five pages, he should take a brightly colored Post-it note, write "Complete bookmark #1," and place it after the first five pages in his book. On another Post-it he writes "Complete bookmark #2" and places it five more pages ahead in his book, and so on. Every time he comes to a Post-it note, he takes out his binder and completes the assigned bookmark.

Step five: the bookmark questions should be changed throughout the novel and can be written to focus on general comprehension (see Exhibit 6.10 for an example) or more specific questions. They can include detailed questions about the novel the student is reading for a more in-depth comprehension check, or you can vary the level of questions according to Bloom's taxonomy for analytical responses. (See literature letters in Chapter 4, Differentiated Thinking Activities; see also Bloom's taxonomy, Exhibit 4.3.)

Exhibit 6-10
Linear Style Contract Sample

SOCIAL STUDIES

Reading Contract

Seventh Grade Social Studies Name and core: _____

Due date: _____

Region of the world and time span: _____

Assigned text: _____

Assigned articles ("title" and pages): _____

ESSENTIAL QUESTIONS:

- What are the sources and outcomes of conflict within and between civilizations over time?
- Which human endeavors have led to the great accomplishments of civilizations?
- How are historical events influenced by physical geography?
- How do the elements of a civilization (religious, political, social, economic) contribute to its successes and failures?

CONTRACT PROCEDURE:

1. (WHOLE CLASS) Review essential questions and complete a KWQ chart in your SSNB with the class for the assigned region of the world.
2. (GROUP) Get together with your group and complete the top portion of this contract.
3. (GROUP) Read your article together as a group, alternating readers while the rest of the group follows along silently.
4. (INDIVIDUAL) In your notebook:
   ○ Complete the reading check questions in complete sentences.
   ○ Define and use each vocabulary term in an original sentence.
5. (GROUP) Come back together as a group to discuss the essential questions. Decide on at least one to answer, and develop a thorough response to record in your notebook and report back to class.
6. (GROUP or WHOLE CLASS) Be prepared to lead a class discussion on the information you learned, using the essential questions as your guide.

I understand the assignment and my individual responsibilities. I will complete the contract to the best of my ability.

Student signature and date:

Exhibit 6-11
Reading Bookmark Contract

TITLE:_____

AUTHOR:_____

Directions: place your "bookmarks" (sticky reminders) _____ pages apart in your book.

    Place bookmark number 1 on page _____ Due date: _____

    Place bookmark no. 2 on page _____. Due date: _____
    TEACHER CONFERENCE

DATE: _____.

    Place bookmark no. 3 on page _____. Due date: _____

    Place bookmark no. 4 on page _____. Due date: _____
    TEACHER CONFERENCE

DATE: _____

    Read your book. When you get to one of the bookmarks, stop and write the answer to the question on this paper. Each question must be completed by the due date.

    Bookmark no. 1 Due date: _____ Page no. _____
    Describe the setting of your book. Where does the story take place? What words did

the author use to describe the setting? _____

_____

    Bookmark no. 2 Due date: _____ Page no. _____
    Who is the main character in your book? What does this character look like? How old is this character? How does this character act (shy, tough, polite, rude, etc.)?

_____

    Bookmark no. 3 Due date: _____ Page no. _____
    What is the conflict in the story? Predict how you think the conflict will be resolved.

_____

    Bookmark no. 4 Due date: _____Page no. _____

    Would you have made different choices or the same ones as from those the main character has made so far? Why or why not? Justify your answer with examples from the story.

_____

_____

_____

In this chapter, we have emphasized the flexible nature of contracts and menus. Students enjoy the responsibility and choice involved in these assignments as they work at their ability levels and consequently feel successful. Because contracts, menus, and tiered assignments are an appropriate level of challenge, students also succeed at mastering grade-level standards. An additional benefit is that the time spent on these differentiated assignments allows students to work individually or with a partner, freeing up the teacher for small-group or individual reteaching or enrichment instruction.

Chapter Seven

Assessment as a Grading Tool

The foremost complex issue of assessment is grading. When we began differentiating curriculum, our school was still using a traditional grading system. We established rubrics for assessment and shared them with the students up front. We laid out clearly what a student needed to do to achieve an A, B, C, and so on. Points or percentage scales guided the grade. But questions arose: What about the students working in a modified curriculum? How do we grade them? For students with IEPs, we often averaged the individual student's effort with the final academic proficiency. The reasoning was that so many of these kids may never be stellar students but they work hard, so we have to give them credit for their dedication, lest we crush their spirits.

It was a valid concern when some teachers expressed that this wasn't really fair, equating an IEP student's grade of B with a non-IEP student's grade of B: What message are we sending the students with solid academic performance who also try very hard? Are we doing a disservice to those kids who, some day out in the real world, will recognize that they aren't really B students? It does make you think.

Our conversations made us start to think seriously about our grading philosophy. We surveyed the staff about what the purpose of grading is, about how important effort is in school, and what effect it should have on grading. We talked about what an A is, a B, a C, and we found the grades to mean surprisingly different things to many intelligent people! So we read. Over the summer, a group of our staff read Robert J. Marzano's *Transforming Classroom Grading* and Ken O'Connor's *How to Grade for Learning: Linking Grades to Standards,* two books on standards-based grading. After reading them, Maureen wanted to apologize to every student to whom she had ever assigned a grade. Who knows how many students we have set up over our own careers for a let-down later in their educational careers, because our standard for an A is not the same as another person's standard. She relates this example:

I taught an undergraduate education class at the local university one semester. When I returned the first assignment, a student requested a conference with me about her grade. She was irate because she had not received an A. I reiterated as gently as possible that I felt she did not show the depth of analysis I expected in the assignment, per the directions, examples, and rubric I had provided. Her response: "But I worked so hard on it!" She was very angry, and I told her she was more than welcome to consider my suggestions for improvement and turn the assignment back in, but she never did. How could a college student, I wondered, believe that simply trying hard would be enough to earn an A?

After reading both Marzano and O'Connor, I no longer wondered. Think about it: if, classroom to classroom, grade to grade, teacher to teacher, we do not have a common philosophy about the purpose of grades and what they represent, why do we place so much importance on grades in our public school system? There is absolutely no consistency.

We believe that the purpose of grading is to communicate to the student and her family how she is progressing, growing, and performing. According to those authors, however, a midterm grade of B in reading, for instance, tells the family very little about how proficient the student is with regard to specific reading standards. Does she have a broad vocabulary, understanding Latin and Greek roots? Does she comprehend seventh grade reading material? Can she analyze literature in a highly critical way?

Standards-Based Grading

To avoid such vague communication, our staff have adopted standards-based grading, which was a difficult change for everyone who grew up in the traditional grading system and learned to accept a grade for its letter worth—however inconsistent. But we believe that this system is better for students and families, because it affords a clearer picture of what a student knows and where she is on the scale of learning.

In the differentiated classroom, the standards-based grading system alleviates previous concerns about "fair" grading. Since all students are learning the same standards (though perhaps in different ways), the same rubric applies to all students. Furthermore, we have implemented a separate "effort" category in all classes schoolwide, with grade-level teams establishing criteria for outstanding, satisfactory, and unsatisfactory effort on assignments.

Sometimes an end-of-the-unit test is called an assessment, and it refers to how proficient students are in various standards. We have created a rubric that is used schoolwide, and now even students with IEPs—whose goals are written in standards language anyway—have the same criteria. Special education teachers can easily determine effort or proficiency without having to even consult with the general education teacher.

Assessment and Reassessment

Assessment, the term we now use for grading, is still meant to guide our teaching. It is also used as a measurement that truly explains what a student does or does not know. Our staff have embraced the notion that a student should have an opportunity to try again and take a reassessment if he does not score proficiently the first time.

Worksheet 7-1
Plan of Study

This is an agreement between student and teacher to help improve understanding of an important concept or unit of study. The student agrees to complete practice work listed below to increase understanding. Once this is completed, the teacher agrees to reassess the student at the time, date, and place listed here.

Student name:

_____

Teacher name:

_____

Subject area:

_____

Assessment to be retaken:

_____

Practice to be completed by student to increase understanding and work toward mastery:

_____

_____

_____

_____

Reassessment:

Date: _____   Time: _____

Place:_____

I agree to complete the practice work listed above by the date agreed on.

Student signature: _____   Date:_____

I agree to reassess student for understanding and mastery.

Teacher Signature: _____

Date:_____

I understand that student needs to complete this practice work in order to be reassessed.

Parent Signature: _____   Date:_____

Given this opportunity, the student must show how he is going to learn the material again before taking the reassessment. He cannot simply ask to take it again because he did not pass it the first time (perhaps because he didn't prepare, or perhaps because he did prepare but simply did not perform well). This emphasizes for students that we value what they learn, not what their final grade is. Learning is what's genuinely important, and the assessment score should be an accurate reflection of that. Therefore, we give students a plan of study. Our colleague Julie Giannini-Previde created the format our staff now use schoolwide.

To prevent memorization of answers (which does not demonstrate content mastery), the reassessment would not have to be the exact same assessment as the first time. It could perhaps be in the same format, such as multiple choice or essay with new questions. Or it could be the same questions in another format. In either case, the information must be the same for it to be a true reassessment. Students, parents, and teachers have to remember that the purpose of education is not merely a final grade but acquisition of knowledge: "[We] can differentiate the pace of instruction and be flexible about the time required for student mastery. Just as we would never demand that all humans be able to recite the alphabet fluently on the first Monday after their 3rd birthday, it goes against all we know about teaching tweens to mandate that all students master slope and y-intercept during the first week of October in grade 7" (Wormeli, 2006, p. 17).

Family Communication

Families are as much a part of our learning community as are educators and students. We keep in touch with parents in a variety of ways, technologically and in person. The online program Edline (www.edline.net) allows us to have ongoing communication with families. This is a Website that students and their families can access with private codes to view the school calendar, class assignments, and class performance. Our computer lab is open to the public once a week for four hours in the afternoon and evenings. We also email frequently. Schoolmaster, a software product from Olympia Computing, is also used schoolwide and allows all staff to access family information, including contacts and phone numbers. We can log in notes of conversations, helpful for other staff members, with common students. Families and teachers can be in constant touch through these technological support systems.

Not only do teachers post homework assignments on Edline each week but also at the beginning of the year each student receives a McKinleyville Middle School "Comet Planner" for recording daily homework assignments. This is helpful for families who do not have access to a computer, and the planner can also serve to help parents communicate in writing with staff. In addition, twice each year students conduct a student-led conference, in place of the traditional parent-teacher conference. This is a time for students to prepare and present in the school setting with their families their best work and reflections on performance. It has proved to be a positive experience for families who might otherwise never see or discuss their children's progress.

Most recently, we have been holding parent forums, encouraging feedback on a newly adopted standards-based grading approach. Our constant efforts at parent outreach encourage partnership and collaboration among all the players involved in the learning experience: students, parents, and educators.

Part Two

Exit Card

1. Which differentiation strategy will you try to apply in your own classroom within the next month?

2. How would you describe your grading philosophy?

3. How can you and your staff begin a dialogue about your grading philosophies?

Part Three

Implementing a *Schoolwide* Program

Chapter Eight

Essential Administrative Support

Most authorities agree that effective organizational change requires that administrators assign the highest priority to collaboration in the schools.

Gable, Korinek, and McLaughlin (2004)

Had it not been for the support and encouragement of McKinleyville Middle School principal Dale McGrew, Mindy might never have considered exploring the integration model. Yes, she is the one who identified the problem with the system. But she needed a principal who supported the academic needs of students as well as her professional needs. He listened to her and trusted her to investigate and pilot the integration program. He sent her to conferences and granted release time for planning as well as for writing proposals. He worked out a schoolwide schedule that would enable Mindy, Julie, and their students to pilot the program, without affecting other teachers and students who were not involved. He also had a long-term vision: to implement the program schoolwide.

Richard DuFour writes: "Principals foster this structural and cultural transformation when they shift their emphasis from helping individual teachers improve instruction to helping teams of teachers ensure that students achieve the intended outcomes of their schooling. More succinctly, teachers and students benefit when principals function as learning leaders rather than instructional leaders" (2002, p. 13).

Dale McGrew was principal of McKinleyville Middle School until he retired in 2002. This is just one principal's story of how systematic change began. His vision and willingness to take risks in the best interest of students have been major influences on the dynamic structure of our current system.

Dale McGrew's Story

Mindy Fattig, one of our special education teachers, came to me in the middle of her first year at McKinleyville Middle School. She expressed frustration with the current model for providing services to our identified students with learning disabilities. These students were placed in their own three-period core class and math class on the basis of their individual education plan (IEP). The core focused on reading, language arts, history and social studies, grades six through eight. Mindy was frustrated by lack of student achievement, low student self-esteem, and classroom management issues within the LD core. She did not believe that the program met the overall needs of the students and felt that she could not continue to teach in the program as it currently existed. I shared Mindy's frustration with the program and the failure to adequately meet student needs. I asked her to research the issue and come to me with ideas for improving our LD service delivery model.

I'm not sure Mindy realized at that time the level of risk takers that surrounded her at McKinleyville Middle School. In becoming a six-through-eight middle school (having changed from a kindergarten-seven-eight), the reflective staff effected a continuous change process. The philosophy of "what doesn't work, doesn't work, and more of what doesn't work still doesn't work" helped staff to sustain program strengths and focus on fixing what doesn't work. Mindy's desire to change something that didn't work into something that did work fit right in with existing school culture. Consequently I never questioned her desire to seek system change.

Mindy went to a California (Region J) special education conference, and to the CalSTAT conference in North Lake Tahoe. On the basis of her experiences at the conferences and her discussions with other school sites, she recommended that we "fully include" our students with learning disabilities into the general education classes. Because of Mindy's enthusiasm for a full-inclusion program, my counselor and I attended a CalSTAT conference in San Diego focused on full inclusion. The three of us agreed that the most responsible way to meet our students' needs would be through such a program. Unlike our current program and the traditional pull-out model, we felt it was critical that the students with learning disabilities and the special education teacher work and learn together in the general education population setting. Special education teachers would collaborate and co-teach with general education teachers to modify and differentiate instruction to meet the needs of *all* students.

Because we wanted to be successful and target a certain group of kids, our inclination was to start small, with one willing teacher. The special education teacher would be assigned to two core classes, one in the morning and a second in the afternoon, with the same general education teacher. There would be roughly ten special education students in each core class.

In the spring of that year, I took six teachers to the California League of Middle Schools conference. We traveled in a single van for six hours, which allowed time for extended discussion on school-related issues. One point of discussion was full inclusion and use of differentiated instruction in the classroom. As a result of the conference experience and the discussions, we had one of our eighth grade core teachers volunteer to implement the full inclusion model in her classroom. We had what we needed to pilot the program for the following year. The success of the pilot led to core teachers volunteering at the other grades, and the program expanded to serve all students with learning disabilities at all grade levels.

The Success at McKinleyville Middle School

As schoolwide implementation of an integrated resource program became reality at McKinleyville Middle School, administration provided the support necessary for educators to sustain truly effective collaboration. Our district created professional development opportunities over the summers. During the school year, we received occasional release time for planning. As our program continues to expand, planning time is a critical factor for its success. Administrators must permit release time for teams and cover substitute teacher costs. Half-days once per trimester, for instance, are helpful for long-term planning. Administration must also be willing to create schedules that allow teamed teachers to collaborate during the regular school day.

Because of the powerful nature of what we were seeing as we increasingly worked as teams, we found planning time was critical to creating and maintaining successful collaboration. Reorganizing the schedule would ensure consistent and continued collaboration. After five years, teacher leaders worked with the administration to reorganize the schedule so that we had common prep periods by subject areas.

Now, we spend anywhere from one hour per week to thirty minutes every day collaborating. Collaboration time includes curriculum mapping (both long- and short-term); discussing the need for differentiation and creating lessons; and most important, reflective teaching. For us, collaboration time is sacred time. Different configurations will suit certain site needs better than others, but it is essential to prioritize and maintain collaboration time if it is to be effective. The energizing effect of collaborating with peers is well worth the time and effort for teachers and ultimately for student achievement.

The success at McKinleyville Middle School can be attributed to several factors:

- First, there was frustration with the current model and desire to do something that better met the needs of our students.
- Second, there was action by the staff to determine how things might work better. For change to occur, there needs to be frustration with what is, a desire to do it better, and action leading to a new way of doing business.
- Third, our change was teacher driven and not top down.
- Fourth, the model continued to evolve (and still does today) according to all students' needs.

- Fifth, the staff were trained in the use of differentiated instructional techniques and Richard Curwin's "Discipline with Dignity" model.
- Sixth, the program required no additional cost or staff, just reallocation of existing personnel and a focus on staff development.

Finally, the change was done in small steps over a period of several years.

There are a number of things a school principal can do to facilitate changing an existing special education program to a full-inclusion model:

- First, and most important, trust your staff. Teachers are intrinsically motivated and want to do what is best for their students. If your staff is satisfied with the status quo, it is very difficult, though certainly not impossible, to change the current practices.
- Give staff the opportunity to create a new vision by attending workshops, visiting successful sites, and talking to the staff members involved in a full-inclusion program. For the guidance and support provided by CalSTAT, McKinleyville Middle School is eternally grateful.
- Supply staff with the ongoing training necessary to successfully implement changes by developing onsite experts.
- Focus on the core curriculum.
- Focus as well on the use of differentiated instruction to meet the needs of diverse students.
- Start small, with individuals who have bought into the concept.
- Expand the program after demonstrated success and as teacher interest develops.

Supportive and Respectful Administration

Successful change depends on administrators acting as partner professionals who are willing to support innovative ideas in teaching. When Mindy approached Dale and told him she would resign if she couldn't make a change, he asked, "What do you suggest?" She already had the mind-set that she could make change happen, and for valid reasons. She had identified the problems and approached her administrator. He opened the door for her by giving the green light to go out and research other special education programs. He extended to her the emotional and financial support she needed to be successful, because he respected her as an educator who knew best what her students needed.

A pitfall to watch out for with a new collaborative model is a top-down, administration-imposed program. Even the most professional teacher and seasoned veteran wants feelings and ideas to be valued as part of an evolving program. We don't like things being forced on us when we believe we know what is best for children. Administrators need to invite the staff to be part of a journey that will prove to be gratifying for everyone involved. Everyone has a stake in the collaborative experiment. Everyone should have a say in how it can work. A fun professional development story that inspires change is *If You're Riding a Horse and It Dies, Get Off*, by Jim Grant, Char Forsten, and Nathan Bundy (1991).

If your administrator is less than supportive, and if you have exhausted every diplomatic means of trying to sway his opinion in the direction of positive change, we suggest you begin sharing your vision with school board members. Invite them into your room; have coffee with them. Convince them that it is in the students' best interest that your administrator begin to support change.

Chapter Nine

Reflections on Making Change Happen

*What is clearly required to alter the status quo is a
sincere desire to change and a firm commitment to
weather the inevitable storms as change occurs.*

Marzano, Pickering, and Pollack (2001)

Our experiences during Dale McGrew's tenure and since then have taught us that a number of conditions are crucial to successfully implementing a collaborative, co-teaching model. Hopefully you will identify some areas of strength that will encourage you on your path to implementing your own collaborative, co-teaching model. Don't be frustrated by areas of weakness. How often have you told your own students, "We can only ask that you try your best" or "We all have strengths and weaknesses"? Consider this a chance to beef up those areas that need improvement.

Teachers Can Make Change Happen

Although many teachers we have worked with across the nation were reluctant to take on the changes involved in implementing a collaborative and co-teaching model, most of them one year later would choose never to return to teaching in isolation. One general education teacher, Kris Herstein from Sanger High School in Sanger, California, has this to say about her first-year experience working with a co-teacher: "[Collaboration] has made me a better teacher. When I am planning and preparing curriculum, I am looking from the perspective of the special education student. Scaffolding, prewriting, idea generating, yes that is for the special education student, but it helps all of my students. It has made me a better teacher for all students that need support. It would be hard to imagine teaching without collaboration."

"Faculties must stop making excuses for failing to collaborate," according to DuFour, Eaker, and DuFour (2005). "Few educators publicly assert that working in isolation is the best strategy for improving schools. Instead they give reasons why it is impossible for them to work together: 'We just can't find the time.' 'Not everyone on the staff has endorsed the idea.' 'We need more training in collaboration.' But the number of schools that have created truly collaborative cultures proves that such barriers are not insurmountable."

A Healthy, Positive, Can-Do Attitude

Success depends on a shared vision among staff. We believe it is our responsibility as educators to make sure that every student in our school is learning and growing. It is our responsibility, and indeed a *privilege* to have the opportunity to develop curriculum and teaching strategies that ensure our students learn and grow. It is downright *irresponsible* to buy into excuses, such as, "We cannot collaborate or co-teach because the schedule will not allow it to happen." Do not let bus and bell schedules influence what you do! Rick DuFour (2004) reminds us that this is the very worst kind of cop-out. Instead, we must ask ourselves, "What is our school's vision?" and "How well are we teaching our kids?"

"How do we know that they are learning and growing?"
"Who made the bus and bell schedules in the first place?"
"Why can't we change *them* instead of compromising our students' education to suit the bells and buses?"

We are also responsible for addressing certain legal requirements: Are we meeting mandated educational resource requirements, such as those of the Williams Law (Equal access to curriculum, California, Senate Bill 550, 2004)? Are we addressing upcoming response-to-intervention structural recommendations (Research-based intervention strategies for students performing below grade level in various disciplines; Individuals with Disabilities Education Act, or IDEA, 2004)? Are the increasing number of special education students and the services needed for them encroaching on our general funds?

Identify your purpose and vision as an educator. Identify your obstacles, strategize ways to overcome them, and take one small step. You can do this on your own, with one partner, with a small group, or best of all with the entire staff. If you want to attempt to change your current school model, begin by working with the people who share your positive outlook. Eventually the can-do attitude will win over any resisters.

Willing Colleagues

Success depends on working for change *first* among those who are willing to take a risk. A sure way to fail in changing your school's model is to attempt to pilot a co-teaching model by imposing it on others. We have met a number of teachers who have complained that they were not involved or consulted in the process of changing over to a collaborative or co-teaching model. When administration forced the model on teachers—assigning teaching partners and handing over unfamiliar schedules at the beginning of the year—they didn't buy in. To implement and sustain a working and evolutionary program requires that all participants hold a stake in its success.

It was no fluke that Mindy first piloted the integrated program with Julie. Julie had experience with an integrated program at her previous school, and she was willing to work with Mindy to develop a program at our site. Both women were passionate and willing to put in extra time to make it happen, both were willing to take a risk that it might be difficult, and both were willing to support the other. They both believed that this would be the best thing for all of *their* kids. *Their* kids. Not Mindy's, and not Julie's, but *their* kids. They worked closely throughout the school year, reflecting and collaborating on curriculum, co-teaching differentiated lessons, and assessing student progress. Their energy was contagious, and they produced a model that the rest of the staff could follow.

Mindy knew that the integrated, co-teaching model would be successful if, the following year, the second special education teacher on staff and several other core teachers volunteered to participate in the program. Indeed, they were eager to collaborate and co-teach, to have a partner to bounce ideas off of throughout the day. After much persistence and extremely challenging schedule changes, such collaboration is now the norm throughout our entire school. Grade-level teams meet daily, despite the excuses for many years that the lunch schedule made it impossible. Our colleagues will never buy that excuse again.

Implement Gradually, Reflect, Adjust

As Dale knew before we even began, success depends on starting small. The initial pilot was successful because Julie and Mindy worked so closely as true partners, in one content area at a single grade level. Once the rest of the staff bought in, we decided to start with the core program only, where students spend three periods of their day for language arts, reading, and social studies. By the second year and implementation of the model throughout our entire core department, our special education students were divided among the core classes, grades six through eight. Our special education teachers, Mindy and Holly, each worked with three or four general education teachers at two grade levels in three or four classrooms. We had not yet implemented the common prep period, so our pacing and lessons varied widely from class to class. You can only imagine how overwhelming it was for Mindy and Holly to keep up with what was happening from day to day, helping to differentiate lessons and assessments for all of these different classes.

Sanger High School experienced a similar situation when they first implemented a co-teaching model. At Sanger, one special education teacher works with each department. "We had three special education teachers go on blood pressure meds after the first year. They were spread too thin and didn't utilize their time effectively," reports Sanger Assistant Principal JoDee Marcellin.

Establishing systems and differentiating curriculum when first getting started requires time above and beyond the regular school day. Teachers who begin working in a collaborative or co-teaching model must be willing to put in that extra time. The payoff is well worth it when you see students feeling and being successful, and when you experience a renewed joy for teaching in general.

Resources

Newly teamed teachers need adequate resources to which they can refer. We found successful collaboration models through our work with CalSTAT. Teachers from around California who are working in a collaborative model are able to share successes and failures in order to improve programs. Marilyn Friend's models of co-teaching (2002) are a continued source of guidance. Our most surprising and inspirational resource is our colleagues. We draw on one another's individual strengths as educators every day. At one time, these strengths were shared only with students in our isolated settings, but now we seek out expertise next door, down the hall, and in staff meetings.

You will find colleagues (administrators too) who have taught your grade level or subject and are likely to have plenty of ideas to help you with a new lesson, modifications, or engaging projects they no longer use. Perhaps you could request that your administrator set aside time during a staff meeting for lesson-share time.

If you are fortunate enough to have one, seek out your gifted-and-talented coordinator, as well your special education teachers, all of whom are invaluable resources. Invite them into your classroom and ask for tips on more effective teaching strategies, how to reach that one child you cannot reach, or lesson ideas, or ask them to co-teach for a period (or an entire day).

If you have a university nearby, contact college students for help. You might even be able to establish a tutoring program for them to earn units. If you teach in an elementary school, contact the middle or high school kids to come into your classes for credit. Better yet, if that local university has a credential program, mentor a student teacher and induct her into the world of co-teaching from the get-go, as we have done with our local university, Humboldt State.

On a practical level—and this is a crucial element in differentiating curriculum—your students deserve access to materials they can actually read at an appropriate level. Contact the teachers and librarians in your district (via email or form letter in the spring) at higher and lower levels for books they no longer use or can recommend you use. These might supplement a classroom library or a particular unit of study. Your county office of education or local library could help with this too. Tap into all those sample books you have stored away in the staff room or your classroom closets for ideas about modifying or accelerating learning experiences. Most of them are brand new and have lots of great ideas worth trying. Local bookstores might pass along used books that come in, if you simply drop by occasionally. Don't forget your students and their families; they might have plenty of books of their own that they no longer use and are willing to donate. Differentiating reading sources is a key component of differentiation (see Part Two). Collect various levels of reading every chance you get.

Co-Teaching in the Integrated Classroom

Our Integration Program has grown and evolved, and it is now implemented schoolwide with overwhelming success. As we continue with it, most important in our daily collaboration is the gratification we feel as we see the joy of learning return to our students' faces, as well as to our own. Mindy says:

> As I continue to co-teach with my colleagues year after year, I am continuously evolving and growing as a professional. I see new, exciting lesson plans and ideas generated between the two of us. The students receive the benefit of differing perspectives and approaches to teaching and learning. They see their co-teachers asking for clarification, admitting mistakes, and congratulating each other on lessons. They also see the smiles on our faces as we observe students using the same teamwork with each other, regardless if they are learning-disabled, gifted, or somewhere in between. We are all here to learn, we are all here to support each other, and we are all here to enjoy learning and middle school in the process.

Glossary

Advanced grade level (AGL)   Students considered to be advanced for a specific grade-level skill or standard, determined through preassessment.

Assessment   Ongoing formal and informal evaluation of student progress. A tool for determining where your students are in their individual learning, it serves as a starting point for instructional planning.

Community building   Ongoing fostering of acceptance and understanding of classroom diversity.

Compacting   An opportunity for students who demonstrate through preassessment that they are ready to delve deeper or faster into the grade-level content.

Contract   An instructional and learning tool that requires students to acknowledge their responsibility to complete the assignment within a given time.

Differentiation   Reflective and responsive teaching that challenges every learner appropriately.

Flexible grouping   Varying arrangements of grouping (by number, ability, learning preference, or style) that maximize student learning opportunities.

Foundational level (*)   Students who perform below the grade-level standard for a specific skill or activity, determined through preassessment.

GATE   Gifted and talented education.

General education (GE) class   Typical mixed-ability classroom, non-IEP, but may include students with 504 plans. *504* refers to section 504 of the Federal Rehabilitation Act, the purpose of which is to provide accommodations for GE students with identified disabilities, though not severe enough to qualify for an IEP.

Grade level (GL)   Students performing at the appropriate grade-level standard for a specific skill or activity, determined through preassessment.

Heterogeneous grouping   Grouping by mixed learning preferences, interests, random selection, or ability.

Homogenous grouping   Grouping by similar learning preferences, interests, or ability.

Integrated resource program (IEP)   Integrating resource students into the general education classes.

Menu   An instructional and learning tool that offers students choice within teacher-designated parameters. Students complete a combination of teacher-assigned "must do's" and student-choice "choose to do's."

Readiness level   A student's ability level for a specific skill or activity, determined through preassessment.

Resource   Student who qualifies for an individualized education plan (IEP) with mild or moderate cognitive disabilities. Currently does not include moderately or severely disabled students.

Tiered assignment   An ability-driven instructional and learning tool. Following preassessment, the teacher establishes foundational, grade-level, and advanced grade level groups for a particular content standard. The teacher then determines appropriate skills, resources, and end products for each group so that each student may maximize his or her individual learning potential.

Annotated Bibliography

This is a list of suggestions to help get you started in building a professional library for collaboration, co-teaching, and differentiation.

Association of Supervision and Curriculum Development. *At Work in the Differentiated Classroom: Planning Curriculum and Instruction.* Videocassette. Shows a truly differentiated classroom run by a reflective and responsive teacher. Five-to-fifteen-minute segments covering assessment, essential questions, community building, flexible grouping, and more. Includes interviews with Carol Ann Tomlinson.

Barton, Linda G. *Quick Flip Questions for Critical Thinking.* Dana Point, Calif.: Edupress, 1997 (www.edupressinc.com). Keep this convenient tool at your fingertips! Based on Bloom's taxonomy, this four-by-six-inch flip book covers key words and critical thinking questions that you can refer to in planning.

Clark, Barbara. *Growing Up Gifted: Developing the Potential of Children at Home and at School.* Upper Saddle River, N.J.: Prentice Hall, 2001 (6th ed.). Covers emotional, social, and academic needs and applications for the gifted child.

Dickinson, Thomas S. *We Gain More Than We Give: Teaming in Middle Schools.* Westerville, Ohio: National Middle School Association, 1997. The importance of a schoolwide mission and teaming is addressed in this collection written by more than twenty educators. Includes portraits of teams at work in schools.

Dieker, Lisa A. *Co-Teaching Lesson Plan Book* (semester version). Whitefish Bay, Wis.: Knowledge by Design, 2002. This book examines the various models of co-teaching and how they may present themselves in the classroom.

DuFour, Richard, and National Educational Service. *How to Develop a Professional Learning Community: Passion and Persistence.* Videocassette. Bloomington, Ind.: National Educational Service, 2002. This is a truly inspirational and fun video for staff development.

DuFour, R., and others, and National Educational Service. *Let's Talk About PLC: Getting Started.* Videocassette. Bloomington, Ind.: National Educational Service, 2004. Addresses professional learning communities as the most effective means of ensuring student learning.

DuFour, R., and Eaker, Robert. *Professional Learning Communities at Work: Best Practices to Enhance Student Achievement.* Bloomington, Ind.: National Educational Service, 1998.

DuFour, R., Eaker, R., and DuFour, Rebecca. *On Common Ground: The Power of Professional Learning Communities*. Bloomington, Ind.: National Educational Service, 2005. Both of the DuFour and Eaker works offer framework and strategies for improving collaboration at your school site. We consider the advice of these authors to be invaluable.

Friend, Marilyn. *Interactions: Collaboration Skills for School Professionals*. Boston: Allyn and Bacon, 2002. The main focus of Friend's book is to offer skills for educators to foster a collaborative environment.

Grant, Jim, Forsten, Char, and Bundy, Nathan. *If You're Riding a Horse and It Dies, Get Off*. Peterborough, N.H.: Crystal Springs Books, 1999. We have used this satirical picture book in a number of professional development workshops to motive groups to make change happen.

Gregory, G. H., and Chapman, C. *Differentiated Instructional Strategies: One Size Doesn't Fit All*. Thousand Oaks, Calif.: Corwin Press, 2002. Practical and concise, this book addresses how to create a climate for learning, knowing, and assessing your learners; adjusting, compacting, and grouping strategies; and approaches for differentiated classrooms. Includes many reproducibles.

Harwell, Joan M. *Complete Learning Disabilities Handbook*. Paramus, N.J.: Center for Applied Research in Education, 2001. Provides current information, practical suggestions, and lessons for meeting the needs of students with learning disabilities.

Heacox, Diane. *Differentiating Instruction in the Regular Classroom: How to Reach All Learners, Grades 3–12*. Minneapolis: Free Spirit, 2002. Definitely one of our favorites. Heacox not only addresses how to prepare differentiation and make it happen but also presents reproducibles of teaching and learning inventories, including those addressing multiple intelligences, project plans, contracts, reflection, and learning logs, among others.

Johnson, Nancy L. *The Faces of the Gifted*. London: Creative Learning Consultants, 1989. Addresses the characteristics and profiles of gifted children.

Reavis, George H. *The Animal School*. Peterborough, N.H.: Crystal Springs Books, 1999. Another picture book we have used in professional development workshops. It is based on a fable that illustrates the importance of valuing individual learning needs.

Silverman, Linda Kreger. *Upside-Down Brilliance: The Visual-Spatial Learner*. Denver, Colo.: DeLeon, 2002 (www.deleonpub.com). Addresses the challenges that approximately one-third of our students face in primarily auditory-sequential classrooms, and offers many ideas to shift teacher thinking about who and how we really teach. Fun anecdotes.

Tomlinson, Carol Ann. *The Differentiated Classroom: Responding to the Needs of All Learners*. Alexandria, Va.: Association for Supervision and Curriculum Development, 1999. Tomlinson is a differentiation guru, and here she introduces the philosophy of differentiation, the current terminology, and models of it at work.

Tomlinson, C. A. *How to Differentiate in Mixed-Ability Classrooms*. Alexandria, Va.: Association for Supervision and Curriculum Development, 2001. The title speaks for itself. Includes great ideas for presenting differentiation to students to get their buy-in.

Tomlinson, C. A. *Differentiation in Practice: A Resource Guide for Differentiating Curriculum, Grades 5–9*. Alexandria, Va.: Association for Supervision and Curriculum Development, 2003. Tomlinson once again shares her expertise, this time focusing on the middle years.

Tomlinson, C. A., and Demirsky Allan, Susan. *Leadership for Differentiating Schools and Classrooms*. Alexandria, Va.: Association for Supervision and Curriculum Development, 2000. Very accessible text on implementing differentiation schoolwide and districtwide.

Villa, Richard A., Thousand, Jacqueline S., and Nevin, Ann I. *A Guide to Co-Teaching: Practical Tips for Facilitating Student Learning*. Thousand Oaks, Calif.: Corwin Press, 2004. Great for first-time teacher teams.

Winebrenner, Susan. *Teaching Gifted Kids in the Regular Classroom*. Minneapolis: Free Spirit, 1996. Winebrenner, S. *Teaching Kids with Learning Difficulties in the Regular Classroom*. Minneapolis: Free Spirit, 1996. Both of Winebrenner's works include step-by-step strategies, activities, and black-line masters to help you challenge and motivate all students in your classroom. Winebrenner addresses learning styles, multiple intelligences, classroom climate, and student responsibility, to mention just a few of the topics. Her no-nonsense style is fun to read.

Wiggins, Grant, and McTighe, Jay. *Understanding by Design*. Alexandria, Va.: Association for Supervision and Curriculum Development, 1998. Wiggins and McTighe describe and show through teaching and learning vignettes the Backward Design process: identify desired results, determine acceptable evidence, and then plan learning experiences and instruction. It is a practice that goes hand-in-hand with differentiation.

References

Bloom, B., and others. *Bloom's Taxonomy of the Cognitive Domain*. Boston: Allyn and Bacon, 1956.

California Senate. *Equal Access to Curriculum*. S 550. Introduced in Feb. 2003, filed Sept. 29, 2004.

California State Board of Education. *Reading/Language Arts Framework for California Public Schools*. Sacramento: California Department of Education, 1999.

Chrisman, V. "How Schools Sustain Success." *Educational Leadership*, Feb. 2005, *62*(5), 16.

Curwin, R. *Discipline with Dignity*. Upper Saddle River, N.J.: Prentice Hall, 2000.

DuFour, R. "Beyond Instructional Leadership: The Learning-Centered Principal." *Educational Leadership*, May 2002, *59*(8), 12–15.

DuFour, R. *Educational Leadership*. Bloomington, Ind.: National Education Service, 2004.

DuFour, R., Eaker, R., and DuFour, R. *On Common Ground: The Power of Professional Learning Communities*. Bloomington, Ind.: National Education Service, 2005.

Feldman, K., and Kinsella, K. " Narrowing the Language Gap: The Case for Explicit Vocabulary Instruction." Scholastic Professional Paper. New York: Scholastic, 2005.

Friend, M., and Cook, L. *Interactions: Collaboration Skills for School Professionals*. Boston: Allyn and Bacon, 2006.

Gable, Korinek, and McLaughlin. *Collaboration in the Schools: Ensuring Success*. InJ. Choate (ed.), *Successful Inclusive Teaching* (2nd ed.). Boston: Allyn & Bacon, 2004.

Gardner, H. *Multiple Intelligences: New Horizons*. New York: Perseus, 2006.

Grant, J., Forsten, C., and Bundy, N. *If You're Riding a Horse and It Dies, Get Off*. Peterborough, N.H.: Crystal Springs Books, 1999.

Individuals with Disabilities Education Act (IDEA) Reauthorization, 2004.

Marzano, R. J. *Transforming Classroom Grading*. Alexandria, Va.: ASCD, 2000.

Marzano, R. J., Pickering, D., and Pollack, J. *Classroom Instruction That Works*. Alexandria, Va.: ASCD, 2001.

National Board for Professional Teaching Standards. "Our Core Propositions." www.nbpts.org (accessed Mar. 1, 2007).

No Child Left Behind (NCLB) Reauthorization, 2006.

O'Connor, K. *How to Grade for Learning: Linking Grades to Standards*. Arlington Heights, Ill.: Skylight, 1999.

Mocilnikar, L. "Gifted Children and NCLB: No Child Left Behind Except the Gifted Ones." Sept. 19, 2006. (www.Suite101.com, Vancouver, B.C.)

Reavis, George H. *The Animal School.* Peterborough, NH: Crystal Springs Books, 1999.

Teachers Curriculum Institute. *History Alive! Rancho Cordova,* CA, 1999.

Tomlinson, C. A. "Mapping a Route Toward Differentiated Instruction." *Educational Leadership,* 1999, *57*(1), 12–16.

Tomlinson, C. A., and Allan, S. D. *Leadership for Differentiating Schools and Classrooms.* Alexandria, Va.: Association for Supervision and Curriculum Development, 2000.

Wiggins, G., and McTighe, J. *Understanding by Design.* Alexandria, Va.: Association for Supervision and Curriculum Development, 1998 and 2005 (2nd ed.).

Winerip, M. "Learning-Disabled Students Blossom in Blended Classes." *New York Times,* Nov. 30, 2005.

Wormeli, R. *At Work in the Differentiated Classroom: Planning Curriculum and Instruction.* (Videocassette.) Alexandria, Va.: Association of Supervision and Curriculum Development.

Wormeli, R. "Differentiating for Tweens." *Educational Leadership,* Apr. 2006, *63*(7), 14–19.

Index